THE MONOCLE BOOK OF ENTREPRENEURS

How to run your own business and find a better quality of life

First published in the United Kingdom in 2021 by
MONOCLE and Thames & Hudson Ltd,
181A High Holborn, London, WC1V 7QX
thamesandhudson.com

First published in the United States of America in 2021 by
MONOCLE and Thames & Hudson Inc,
500 Fifth Avenue, New York, New York, 10110
thamesandhudsonusa.com

MONOCLE is a trading name of Winkontent Limited

British Library Cataloguing-in-Publication Data
A catalogue record for this book is available from
The British Library

Library of Congress Control Number: 2021934198

For more information, please visit *monocle.com*

This book was printed on paper certified
according to the standards of the FSC®

Edited by *Joe Pickard & Molly Price*
Foreword by *Tyler Brûlé*

———

Designed by *Monocle*
Proofreading by *Monocle*
Typeset in *Plantin*

———

Printed by *Eberl & Koesel GmbH
& Co. KG*

Printed and bound in Germany

ISBN 978-0-500-97118-5

Contents

Foreword

By the time this book comes off press and starts making its way to bookshops and well-stocked kiosks, MONOCLE will be marking its 15th year in business. We started out with an idea focused on delivering solid journalism, smart opportunities and a healthy dose of quality goods and experiences to an international audience. As an editorial start-up the pitch was straightforward, investors understood it and without too much haggling we were able to secure the funds, hire the staff and purchase the resources to bring it to market.

The business plan was sound but not without risk; the money required to go global was not enormous but still significant enough for investors to think twice before transferring cash and the landscape was competitive. Back then having a magazine with some digital add-ons was enough to satisfy not only the needs of potential investors but also readers and advertisers. Shortly after our launch we added a small, rather analogue-style e-commerce business followed by podcasts, a TV series and then shops.

As we broadened our reach we asked ourselves, quite frequently, if these new extensions fitted with our overall strategy? Did they deviate from the original mission? Would investors see them as a distraction? And would these new revenue opportunities be worth the effort? Even though we're well past the start-up phase, there are many days when it feels like we're just getting underway as we move into new areas of business while still relishing the moment a new edition of the magazine or a freshly printed book is delivered from the printers. The simple ritual of cracking open an issue, smelling the paper and examining the print quality is a good gauge as it also reminds us that, at the very heart of our business, we love what we do – being entrepreneurs delivering great content.

Across this book you'll meet owners, innovators, collaborators, dealers and creators from all corners of the world who've built businesses that have become global brands, neighbourhood heroes or are just in the roll-out stage. You will be introduced to enterprises both massive and miniscule that make their customers, employees and owners happy. As we touch down in cities, towns and villages to meet business owners and hear their stories you just might find yourself rethinking where you might want to relocate when you decide to press play on your new project.

And don't forget to keep us in the loop – we want to be the first to write about any new venture inspired by these pages. You can always find us at *info@monocle.com*.

Tyler Brûlé
Editorial Director & Chairman

Introduction

What did you want to be when you grew up? The odds are that these dreams have shifted a little over time, but does your ideal vocation bear any resemblance to what you do today? And for that matter, what might your life look like if you turned your passion into your profession? No, this isn't a job interview. But these are exactly the sort of questions that countless people have asked themselves before taking the plunge and starting something from scratch.

This book is about them – but it could just as easily be about you too if you follow their lead. The people profiled within these pages took different professional paths but they all took risks, learned lessons and occasionally got things wrong. All of them persevered and created companies they are proud of too. Starting a business, whether it's a sustainable farm in Galicia or a design studio in New Delhi, means deciding what to do differently. Each of the 100 companies in our success stories chapter have a value but what unites them is the values of those who started them.

Now for a quick qualifier. This isn't a book about getting rich quick or immediately flipping your firm when the first buy-out offer comes along. Instead, it's about building something meaningful, interesting and with integrity. Remember, you decide what success looks like (and if hours craning over a computer is it). Perhaps you'd be happier earning less

and working in a smaller city. What about being able to cycle to the office or being able to take the time to do the school run? Maybe fulfilment to you means time to travel, the joy of breaking ground on an office in a new city or just doing something better than everyone else? Maybe it's about the money, or the thrill of the deal. That's the beauty of having your own business. You're the boss, you can decide. We're just here to help with a little gentle encouragement, some tips, ideas and inspirations to help you along the way.

One thing to make clear here is that entrepreneurship is rarely the easy option – predictability is for wage-workers. No matter how bright your idea is on paper, you may hit humps in the road. That's why we've amassed a team of more than 50 experts to proffer advice on everything from success to succession (and much more besides) and help shepherd you past the bumpier bits. We can't promise it will be simple but we can guarantee that it won't be dull, and the good you do could ripple outwards to revive a high-street, create a company you're proud of and make something that lasts.

All this begs the question: what do you want to be now you're able to decide for yourself? Well, whether or not you've chosen yet, there's plenty in *The Monocle Book of Entrepreneurs* to get you going.

PART I.

ASK
THE
EXPERTS

Every age has its myths and in business that means the fictional idea of the flawless "founder". The story goes that this genius knew what the world needed and didn't take a jot of advice between eureka and the IPO. Instead, as most entrepreneurs will attest, running your own enterprise takes graft, grit and good luck at the best of times. They'll also tell you that inspiration can come from the most unlikely of places: friends, strangers or chance encounters. Good ideas are everywhere if you're open to them.

Entrepreneurship is an inherently risky business. Many people who start-up fail (often several times) before they find a formula that works. It also requires a suite of skills. Some people are excellent with the sales patter but can't decipher a financial spreadsheet. Others may find growing – and leading – a team their biggest hurdle. As such, launching a company takes humility. Listening to people who have walked the path before can be invaluable. To help, we've amassed advice from those who have learned on the job. Expect pointers on the importance of customer service to naming, branding and building a business that lasts (and the unexpected perks of pooch ownership). Plus some key lessons, ideas and inspiration. Shall we introduce you to your new mentors?

I.
Getting started

You've decided to launch your own business but how do you take a sure-fire idea and turn it into a fully-functioning company? Well, gather round: we have gleaned a few pearls of wisdom from those who have been there, done that and sold the t-shirt.

LIGHTBULB MOMENT
Looking for your bright idea
by Ben Lewin

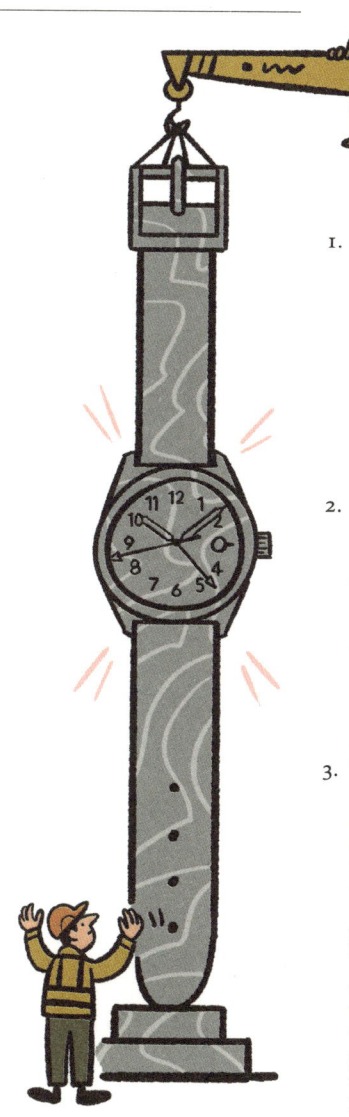

The expert: Lewin is the co-founder of Farer, the producers of a UK-designed Swiss-made watch with a difference.

The lesson: Successful businesses aren't always the result of a groundbreaking idea or revolutionary technology – sometimes a fresh take on an old format is all it takes. But the key is knowing your market and finding a solution to a problem within it.

Just because a market is crowded it doesn't mean there isn't a gap. There's always space to disrupt, you may just need to play a bolder hand to do it. I co-founded British watch brand Farer with Stuart Finlayson, Jono Holt and Paul Sweetenham in 2015. Back then, the established global watch market was going through a rough patch but the second-hand vintage market was booming. Similar to the growth of the classic car market, consumers were looking to the past for unique designs. And they were getting direct access through the digital world. That was our gap. We saw an opportunity to make watches that were inspired by the past yet built for the future. Combining bold design with the very best craftsmanship – and delivering them through our own direct-to-consumer digital channels.

There are a few things we got right. The first one was our relentless focus on creating the Farer design DNA (which drives everything we do). Other things – like the pain of back-end stock systems – we have had to learn the hard way. Looking back now, there are three things that helped us find our gap.

1. **Trends don't last**
   You need more than just a point of view going into your market. You need a great product and every detail across the customer journey has to be an improvement on what your competitors offer. The days where marketing hype succeeds over product quality are long gone. True product-first brands that are ultimately delivering something different and better are winning hands down.

2. **Go where your audience is**
   It's easy to go where the other established brands are and to assume that people will come to you. Instead, we looked a little harder and found a big group of consumers who were being ignored and who wanted a more personal experience with watch brands. So we turned up and talked to them, in-person and digitally. It's impactful when you make that sort of effort.

3. **Build a community**
   You can't do it alone. Breaking into an established market takes time and money but building a band of believers is a powerful thing. Your most-trusted early converts might be only 10 per cent of your customers, but they'll help you find the other 90 per cent. We launched the Farer Club to give our highest-level customers the chance to be part of our journey; as members, they can get their hands on exclusive products and direct access to what we're doing next before anyone else. In return, they tell friends, family and work colleagues about us in a way we could never replicate on our own terms.

It's time to ditch the nine-to-five

by Cyrielle Rigot and Julien Tang

The experts: Rigot and Tang are the co-founders of Riad Jardin Secret, a boutique hotel in Marrakech.

The lesson: Many people dream of leaving the office behind and pursuing something more fulfilling. But how do you find the nerve to actually take the plunge – and what happens next?

In 2015 on a flight back from Marrakech, we asked ourselves: "Why are we leaving?" We both worked in fashion in Paris and had been travelling to and fro between the two cities for years. We'd always wanted a different life – one that was laidback and sustainable – and we'd fallen in love with the energy of Morocco. So we decided to leave our home city and set up a small hotel in Marrakech.

Within two months we were back in Morocco. We had always wanted to host people who share our passion for art, architecture, travel and conversation. We wanted to create a place that represented our vision of hospitality, where creative souls could recharge and be inspired. When we arrived, it was challenging. But we were ready to adapt for our project. We started to visit properties and meet people, walking the streets and knocking on doors. When we came across our riad it was everything we'd dreamed of. From that moment, everything happened very quickly.

Of course, we had doubts when leaving our lives in Paris, but we had confidence in ourselves, our project and our ability to adapt to a new way of life. Today, we rarely feel like we are working – we've never been happier. If you're thinking about leaving it all behind in search of something better, our advice would be to believe in your first instincts. We did and we wouldn't change a thing.

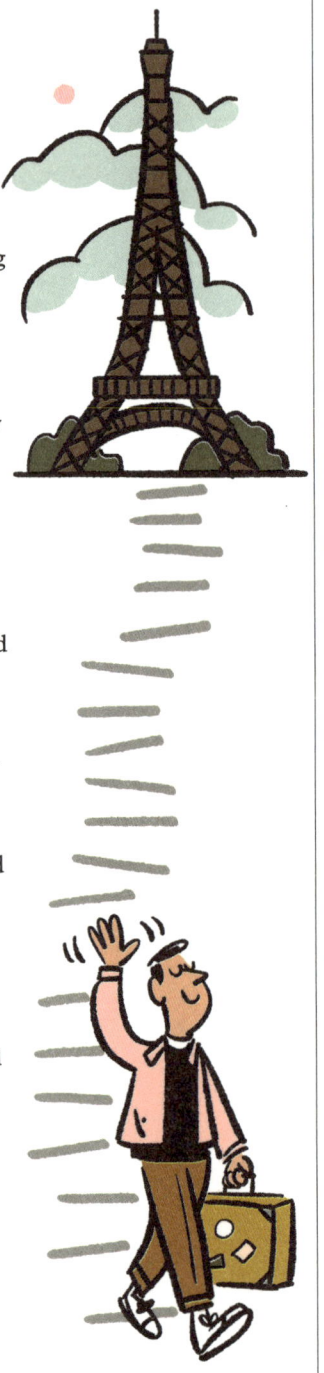

Why I went into business with my mates

by David Allemann

The expert: David Allemann is co-founder of the Swiss running brand On, which he launched in 2010 with friends Caspar Coppetti and Olivier Bernhard.

The lesson: You may enjoy hanging out with them but will your best mate make the best business partner? Much like parenting, growing a business can test any relationship – so make sure yours is a solid one.

A cry comes from the bedroom. It's my seven-month-old daughter. Who will get there first? Will it be me, my wife, the baby's grandma or Zürich's best nanny? As the saying goes, it takes a village to raise a child. And it's no different for my eldest: the running brand On.

The business was born in 2010 out of the friendship of its three founders: myself, Caspar Coppetti and Olivier Bernhard, brought together by our love of running – and the idea of how to re-invent it. The first three years were tough, it was not dissimilar to the demanding days of early parenthood. We experienced a lot of joy in getting the business off the ground and our friendship was the glue that held the vision and the emerging culture together. When we disagreed on important points, the debate could be emotional as things can be between friends. Trust was challenged. At times we wondered whether the partnership would survive. Many start-ups may have seen one or more friends-turned-founders exit at this point. Olivier, Caspar and I chose the opposite: to make more friends. Including myself, there are currently 19 partners parenting On.

But does this work? In my experience, the biggest challenge for a parent is the same as a global company: bandwidth. A group of partners can spread out to go after more missions, make decisions faster, flag risks earlier and beat the classic CEO model.

At On, big decisions are intensely debated with the full partnership. These benefit from diverse viewpoints across genders, seven nationalities and different backgrounds. In fact, I believe that On's diversity is a catalyst for constant innovation and an important part of its success. A wise godfather to the business once told us: "Always treat your partners as your bosses". It's humbling to have 18 of them.

How to think like an entrepreneur
by Stefan Allesch-Taylor

The expert: Professor Stefan Allesch-Taylor CBE is a professor of entrepreneurship at King's College London. He has invested in, co-founded and served as chair or CEO of 100 companies and counting in more than 15 countries.

The lesson: Business schools teach that there are seven key attributes of an entrepreneurial mindset. Allesch-Taylor offers them here (with a twist) drawn from his own experience of more than 30 years in business at the coalface of hundreds of businesses around the world.

1. **Compel**
   Learn to "sell" your product or service. Take every opportunity to talk about it and practise getting people interested. Listen to all feedback, especially the painful. If you're lucky your critics will "write" your elevator pitch. You need to be able to communicate your proposition clearly and effectively. This means the product or service and the business plan itself. You're a salesperson now.

2. **Disrupt**
   What are you doing that's not already being done? Businesses change as markets shift, competitors pop-up and consumers move on. Being an entrepreneur means not being stuck in your ways. You must innovate. Your business exists to provide a compelling solution to a problem (see point 1) and people are looking to you as the founder to keep the business ahead of the competition. Disrupt, pivot, stay focused and stay ahead. You do this by knowing as much about your competitors as you do about your own venture.

3. **Think lean (and agile)**
   Learn how to do things on a shoestring. You need to demonstrate that you know how to do a lot with a little before you are given a lot. This stands true whether it's a small personal loan you're using or a multi-million-pound investment. Wasting money when you could have used your guile to persuade and achieve is a waste of your talent.

4. **Validate**
   Harvard Business School estimates that 43 per cent of all ventures fail because they never had a product or service in the first place. Think about that.

5. **Be resilient**
   Learn how to manage (and even enjoy) the roller-coaster ride and experience defeat without it defeating you. Entrepreneurship is a journey full of wild highs and soul-crushing lows, and if you're not experiencing these, then you're not taking enough (calculative not speculative) risks. You won't always get it right. That doesn't matter.

6. **Build teams**
   The ability to lead, motivate and reward your team is a matter of trial and error. You must nurture these qualities in yourself. It is probably the single most important part of being a successful, and serial, entrepreneur.

7. **Get it done**
   You can have all the projections, plans, financial forecasts and spreadsheets you want, but there comes a time when you need to get your product or service out there. Pontification is your enemy, adapt as you go.

> **TOP TIP**
> Some ventures are instantly profitable – others take a while. Study your sector to know what to expect

A WORD OF ADVICE
from Yoshiharu Hoshino, CEO *of Japan-based hotel chain Hoshino Resorts*

"Remember that there are many more failures than successes when it comes to start-ups. But those who fail aren't always getting something wrong; they may have good ideas and a solid vision, they may just need more time. Too often, people want a quick return – investors might expect a profit in three years. To build something that truly lasts, you have to invest in time and have a long-term commitment."

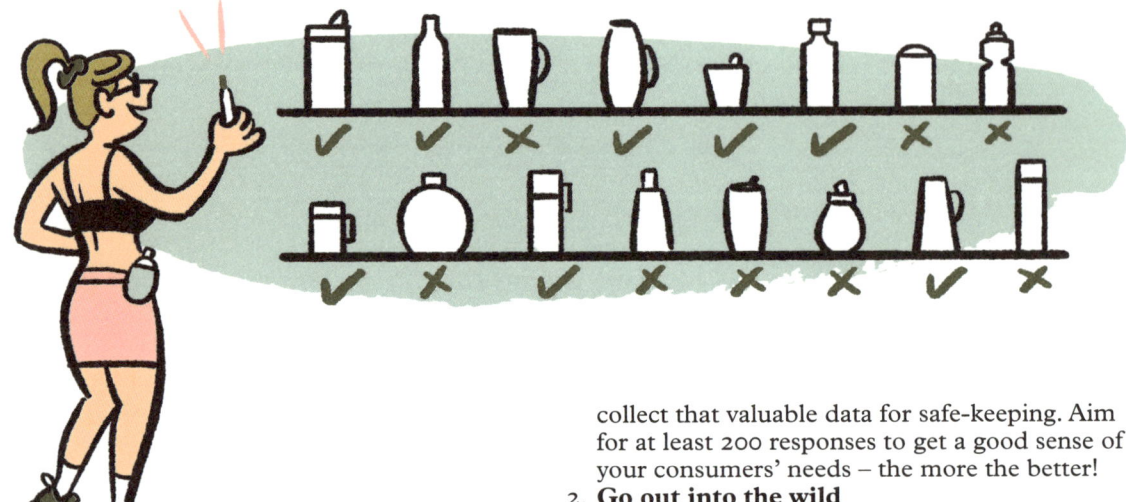

MADE TO MEASURE
Why the customer is always right
by Justin Wang

The expert. Justin Wang is CEO and co-founder of Larq, the business behind the world's first self-cleaning water bottle.

The lesson: You think you've got an idea for a great new product that will solve all your customers' problems. But how can you be sure it's really that good? It's simple – just ask.

The best products are those that are designed to meet the needs of the consumer. Once you adopt this consumer-centric thinking, you'll start making product design and engineering choices that distinguish a good product from a truly outstanding one. Showing your audience that you are open to – and will take onboard – feedback is another recipe for success. In fact, this informed approach was integral to creating Larq's Purevis technology and the brand mission. Staying true to our consumer-centric approach, the priorities of technology and design fall perfectly in line. It's like getting the perfect milk-to-cereal ratio on the first bite. Here's how we did it:

1. **Don't be afraid to tap into your peer group**
   A great idea like yours deserves to proved. Ask your friends, family and their pals for feedback. Use a survey platform to share your idea and collect that valuable data for safe-keeping. Aim for at least 200 responses to get a good sense of your consumers' needs – the more the better!

2. **Go out into the wild**
   It's easy to think that you should have all the answers as a founder, but as an entrepreneur it is important to ask for help when it's needed. At Larq, we tested our early design concepts by standing outside a supermarket and asking the shoppers which water bottle shape they liked best. Despite eventually being asked to leave the premises, we collected invaluable insight at a critical point in our design process. You'd be surprised how many people are willing to help if you simply ask.

3. **Create a community**
   Continued success happens by including like-minded individuals and early adopters who support your brand throughout the process. Odds are, if they've purchased your product then they are invested in the journey. Services such as crowdfunding platform Kickstarter allow you to tap into an existing community who are ready to support innovation and give live feedback. The Kickstarter backers act as a focus group of potential customers since they actually have to put down their credit card details.

4. **Revisit, revise, maintain**
   It's important to remember that as your brand grows, your customers will too and so it's your job to ensure that your great idea doesn't become stagnant. Ask for feedback. While newsletters allow you to speak to your customers, social media can create a dialogue for real-time conversations. If you think something might need a refresh, ask the world at large with a poll. The majority of your customers will be eager to help design the next generation of your product, so don't be afraid to start a discussion with your community.

The art of hiring
by Cherry Swayne

The mentor method
by Sonya Barlow

The expert: Cherry Swayne is the founder of Above & Beyond Recruitment and has supported hundreds of business leaders with the recruitment of their teams.

The lesson: Building a team is a challenging yet rewarding task and creating a scalable, effective hiring process will be a crucial part of achieving fast, sustainable growth for your business.

Define the role
Consider your goals and decide who you need to hire to help you achieve them. Build a comprehensive job description defining their contribution to the business. You should also perform a diversity audit on your workforce and identify where you lack representation.

Create a compelling employer brand
Define your Employer Value Proposition (EVP). This is the employee experience at your organisation, made up of benefits such as health and wellbeing support, company culture, progression opportunities and reputation.

Then tell people about it
Continually communicate your EVP to the wider market as part of your recruitment strategy, even when you're not hiring. Ensure you have an impressive careers page and drive traffic through an active social media presence.

Source talented people
"Build it and they will come"– unfortunately, this is not true when recruiting teams. Your marketing may attract some applications but you will also need to do proactive sourcing. Use your own network initially, then enlist the support of external recruiters for roles that are either urgent or require specialist knowledge to fill.

Screen and interview
Decide how many interview stages you will hold, the format and whether you require a practical test or presentation. Then decide who to involve; ensure a good cross-section of opinion while also choosing those who are positive and sell the company. Make the interview process quick and efficient (no more than two weeks end-to-end). Finally, create a scoring matrix to assess all candidates against the same criteria and minimise unconscious bias.

Onboarding
This should begin when the candidate accepts the job. Include them during their notice period; send them important communications, invite them to social events and allocate them a buddy. Once they've started, take feedback on the recruitment process and use it to make improvements and evolve.

> **TOP TIP**
> Finding the perfect balance between skills and personality can be hard – some roles require more of one than the other

The expert: Sonya Barlow is an award-winning entrepreneur, founder of LMF Network, diversity coach, author of *Unprepared to Entrepreneur* and host of 'The EveryDay Hustle' at BBC Asian Network – plus a mentor herself.

The lesson: The life of an entrepreneur can be a lonely one and sometimes all you need is to talk to someone who's been through it all before – that's where a mentor can step in.

1. **Been there, done that**
   Having a mentor during your entrepreneurial journey is an opportunity to gain access to the knowledge and experience gleaned from someone who has already learned the ropes – and more than likely, weathered a few storms of their own. Entrepreneurial beginners can learn from their mentor's mistakes – and their successful strategies. Those lessons will be invaluable and might help you have an easier path if you listen, learn and allow your mentor to lead by example.
2. **Stay focused**
   One of the most challenging aspects of entrepreneurship is the discipline required to achieve your objectives. A mentor can support you in setting achievable goals and hold you accountable for your progress.
3. **Your biggest fan**
   Entrepreneurship can be a lonely road, with many setbacks, failures and rejections. There will be times when, as an entrepreneur, you will need a cheerleader and confidence booster.

Mentees are not the only ones who benefit from a mentorship programme – I have reaped the rewards of accompanying entrepreneurs on their journey. Guiding others through the jungle that is building your own business has helped me reinforce my particular entrepreneurship style and reconfirm that it was the right path for me.

Mentoring other entrepreneurs has also provided me with a deep sense of fulfilment, especially if they come from underprivileged backgrounds. Representation is hugely important and I hope that through my story, I can encourage more diversity in entrepreneurship and mentoring.

Ask the experts —— Getting started

The benefits of a subscription-based business model
by Josh Lachkovic

The expert: Josh Lachkovic is founder of The Wine List, a subscription service that offers accessible wine education by the month.

The lesson: There's a reason why people love having everything from recipe kits to houseplants delivered to their door on a regular basis – but is the subscription model right for your business?

The last decade has seen subscriptions ride through every part of the so-called tech adoption wave. When I started working in subscriptions in 2014, they were at their first peak. In the two years leading up to that, the snack subscription brand Graze had gone from early adopter obscurity to being in every office in London. Meanwhile recipe delivery box Gousto had launched in 2012, with HelloFresh quick to follow in the UK to much fanfare. The US had seen the viral explosion of Dollar Shave Club inspire dozens of imitators. Everywhere you looked a consumer product was being turned into a subscription.

In the years since, the euphoria has died down. Investors now understand the data better. And for consumers there's more choice than ever. For many, a sense of subscription fatigue has set in. And yet subscriptions – when you consider them simply as a business model – are at an all-time high.

Over the last eight years, I've worked at some of London's fastest-growing subscription businesses – and in 2019 I started my own. When studying for a wine qualification I found the teaching to be archaic, so I started Wine List as a way to help people learn about the craft

in bitesize lessons; each month, students are sent a different chapter with wines to try from home – all via, you guessed it, a subscription. So why then should you start a subscription-based business? Competition is at an all-time high, and the stakes even greater. Here are five things to consider:

1. **Make sure you're something-first, subscription-second**
   Design for the customer problem first, and then the business model second. Adding 'subscription' on to any item probably isn't a winner.
2. **Ask if you're about convenience, curation or something else**
   For convenience, you get essential items delivered (toilet paper for example) while with curation experts choose items for you (think craft beer). Be careful here – if you're following a passion, you might think people want the latter when actually they want the former.

3. **Understand the metrics**
   Subscriptions are brilliant business-wise because customers give you money regularly. But it's not that simple – you have to consider retention, margin and how those things factor against the initial outlay to acquire a customer. Get to know your CPA (cost per acquisition), payback, retention, margin and LTV (loan-to-value).

4. **Do you want investors?**
   A great choice for start-ups and lifestyle businesses, this model provides you with reliable ways of forecasting stock and can help keep overheads to a minimum. But it will also change your ability to acquire customers at scale if you need to break even in the first month.
5. **Launch today**
   If you've got the above sorted, then launch today. Get your idea out there. To get started, pre-sell your subscription box before you've bought stock, and you'll understand quickly whether the product is resonating.

from José Miguel de Abreu, co-founder of Portuguese clothing brand La Paz

"A company is all about the people that make it: the employees, partners, customers, and the community in general. This is why at La Paz we ensure that our employees enjoy the time they spend at work, but also have time to themselves too.

The company is the result of an old friendship between me and co-founder André Bastos Teixeira and our will to turn some of our romantic ideas into something more palpable. Our main motivation was to have the time to do the things we like such as surfing, playing tennis, reading or having a long lunch without having to rush. Now I have the time to do everything I want to do and I love my work."

TOP TIP
As the boss, treat yourself as you would any other employee: be exacting but fair – and show some kindness too

The truth about being your own boss
by Anna Codrea-Rado

The expert: Anna Codrea-Rado is a writer, podcaster and author. Her first book, *You're The Business*, is a practical handbook for anyone who works for themselves.

The lesson: You might think that launching your own company will solve all your boss-based problems but what kind of manager will you turn out to be?

In 2016 I was sitting in a basement office fantasising about a different working life. Back then, I worked for a digital magazine in Brooklyn and I loved what I did but I hated how I was doing it.

I was expected to be at my desk at the same time every day, which also happened to be the same time that the rest of the city was expected to be in their respective offices. So I battled commuter crowds on stuffy subway trains that often broke down. In the office, I sat a few seats away from a guy with a very loud phone voice whose main job, it seemed, was talking on the phone. Struggling to get my work done in the circus of the open-plan office, I asked if I could work from home one day a week. My request was denied.

I blamed everything wrong with my job on bad bosses. It was a boss, after all, who took my flexible working request to their boss, who duly turned it down. It was a boss who set a rigid working hours policy. And it was a boss (no doubt from a private office) who decided staff should sit in an open-plan layout. So, I stopped working for other people and started working for myself. I've now been my own boss longer than I've been anyone else's employee.

It turns out I'm terrible. Sure, I finally approved my work-from-home request but that's where my compassion ends. I've not checked in to make sure I'm taking my holiday days. I've forced myself to work when I've been sick. Nothing is ever good enough for me. I'm a tyrant.

Being self-employed has made me confront my messy relationship with my work. I derive a lot of fulfilment from what I do but I'm also aware of how much of my self-worth I wrap up in it too. I'm enmeshed in my identity as a journalist, not knowing where my job ends and where I begin. I work hard to prove myself – to whom or what I'm not even entirely sure. Looking back now, it was perversely comforting having the spectre of a bad boss to blame for my frustrations when really I was causing my own problems.

The secret of the trade when you work for yourself is that you're not just the boss, you're the whole business. You're the CEO, employee, head of HR and chief financial officer all at the same time. It's a very chaotic working environment but it's also within your power to change the things that aren't working. And if you want your boss to get off your back and give you a break, it's on you.

2.

Brand identity

There's more to branding than a zippy logo: packaging, uniforms, a clever name and even the design of your office space can help your business stand out from the crowd.

Choosing the right name
by Ed Yeoman

The expert: Yeoman is a writer, strategist and head of copy at Winkreative, MONOCLE's sister design agency.

The lesson: You've hit upon that golden idea for a business – but what to call it? The name you choose for your company goes a long way towards defining its success.

First, a confession. I recently became the last person in the world to realise that The Beatles is a pun. It's a weird one but I just never cottoned on to its incorporation of "beat". It's a revelation all the more embarrassing given that it's my job to identify and understand the intricacies and subtleties of what makes a great name. Having come to terms with my mistake, I have decided that it represents something more than humble absentmindedness: it tells us something rather interesting about naming.

I would wager that most people don't notice the finer points of a brand name. They won't care where the words came from and they won't think about etymology, mythology, psychology or any other 'ology that served as inspiration. Does anyone (who isn't Danish) know that Lego means "play well" or that Uniqlo is a portmanteau of unique and clothes? Does anyone out there really care that Nike is the Greek goddess of victory or that Ikea is an acronym of Ingvar Kamprad (its founder), Elmtaryd (the farm where he lived) and Agunnaryd (the village he grew up in)? Yet the origin of these names is important. Along with market positioning and communicating the brand's narrative and values, they create the cohesive story that serves as a foundation for all future work. Beyond that small matter, they also help staff understand the organisation's culture, history and vision for the future. So when it comes to naming your business, you need to know that your name can do two things: attract attention and give you space to grow.

A good place to start is to lay out all the names of the brands in your sector and look for the gap in the market. Branding is about telling a story that nobody else is; if everyone is calling themselves Something & Something, why not call yourself The Something Company? At this point, if you want a name that lasts, you'll need to consider the trickier part: instilling your name with meaning.

Generally we want to feel a sense of honesty and integrity; that there is a certain provenance and an understanding of a wider purpose. Choosing something descriptive and straightforward might reduce your marketing budget in the short-term but, alternatively, that heavily marketed abstract name could help you build a brand that people remember. The name will influence the life and success of a business – getting it wrong could leave you open to ridicule.

Naming a business is an emotional and financial investment, which is why trying to decide on a name can induce a form of business-halting paralysis. Perhaps it's best to take inspiration from some of the biggest names in business. Jeff Bezos decided against calling his online retailer Cadabra and instead chose Amazon because customers kept mishearing the former as "cadaver" over the phone; Apple was named after Steve Jobs came back from a trip to an apple farm; and Häagen-Dazs was a name made up in 1961 by its founders to convey old-world tradition and craft. So there really aren't any limitations apart from your imagination and ability to convince your colleagues of a name's merits. But tread carefully: for every industry-defining winner, there's a Thai Tanic (restaurant), Analtech (pharmaceutical company) and Big Beaver Stump Grinding (by all accounts a highly rated tree removal service in Massachusetts) waiting in the wings.

Two bits of advice to leave you with. First, objectivity is your friend. Second, keep a naming brief to check back on. But the general rule is: if it feels right, it probably is. And if you change your mind you can always rename it. After all, Google was originally called BackRub; there's hope for us all.

The golden rules of naming:

1. **Start wild**
   There will be time for safe ideas later so cut loose and go on a creative safari. At this point every idea should be welcomed, no matter how wild.

2. **Head down the rabbit hole**
   You're only ever one idea away from your Apple, Orange or BlackBerry so explore the fruit section at your supermarket. And don't forget to have a read of that Old Norse dictionary. You never know where you'll find the perfect words.

3. **The eureka moment is rare**
   Good names can be slow burners. Don't decide too quickly: the right name will often need time to percolate.

4. **Be lucky for more than just some**
   Sure, you want to be big in China but have you picked a number or a colour as part of your name? If so you should leaf through those numerous resources devoted to Chinese mythology to learn about what is lucky – and what is not so lucky.

5. **Trends don't last**
   Don't plump for a name that fits the latest fashion if you want it to age gracefully. Name for keeps.

6. **Don't box yourself in**
   Always choose a name that allows for an expanded business, service or product line.

7. **Don't worry about URL availability**
   Modified URLs can work just as well. It's sometimes helpful to split naming ideas into types or constructs so that you're ticking all boxes.

8. **If in doubt, make it up**
   This is generally a good idea if done with care. The trick is to take a word with positive associations that are relevant to your business then change a letter or two – and bingo. Or Bipgo. See? Easy.

> **TOP TIP**
> Naming your business is a bit like naming your child: somehow you can just tell if it sounds off

The business of branding
by Richard Spencer Powell

The expert: Spencer Powell is MONOCLE's creative director. He has branded not only the magazine (and this book) but also our retail division.

The lesson: A company's brand identity should bring its founding values to life – and draw in a few customers too. Just don't forget to have a bit of fun with it.

1. **Research**
   Look at the market, visit similar operations and sample the competition. Keep a record of certain elements that you like: it will help to explain your ideal positioning to any prospective design team. The more direction at the outset the better.

2. **Pick a good agency**
   It is important to have faith in the team that you entrust to design your brand. They are the experts and have both the tools and the eye to create the most alluring package, so it is important to listen to their advice. However, don't allow the creative to go off point and create work that only satisfies their taste. If it doesn't feel right, it probably isn't.

3. **Go beyond the logo**
   When thinking about your company's brand, try to expand the thinking beyond the logo, colour palette, business card and letterhead. Designers will often refer to these items as the basic elements but you don't want to be left with just these. Extra printed material and branded pieces can convey a great deal more.

4. **Application**
   Branding is about application. How you colour, print and position your brand is actually the branding part. A beautiful logo that is too small or disappears two clicks into your website fails to make an impression. Make sure that your brand's palette is as colourful as you want it and that logos and patterns are suitably scaled. Try to think of this in terms of noise volume: some things need to be quieter than others but on certain occasions you need to turn it up.

5. **Further development**
   Think big and test your brand. Things that may seem unlikely at the outset may quickly come into play; additional packaging fixes, collaborative projects or mailing solutions. Your logo, which is largely screen based, may have to be scaled up to live on the side of a delivery van. Test it to see if it works and check it doesn't alter the tone.

6. **Maintenance**
   Make sure you have simple guidelines in place as to how your brand is handled visually. There's room for movement here but not much and the bigger you grow, invariably the more people can, and will, affect the aesthetics. Regular checks should ensure that the appearance stays true to the original design.

Why the design of your office is key to your brand identity

by Josh Fehnert

The expert: Fehnert is MONOCLE's deputy editor. From his desk at Midori House, he can often be seen enjoying the views across the nearby park through sparkling windows.

The lesson: The company HQ should be a palpable representation of your brand values. The interior, and exterior for that matter, should be a place to welcome clients – with not a ping-pong table in sight.

Offices say a great deal more about the businesses we run than most of us care to consider. While not everyone you deal with will be privy to the board report, backroom dealings or bottom line, plenty will experience what you do through the four walls from which you run the show.

A vignette to illustrate my point. A few years ago, Aussie chef and author Bill Granger taught me a trick. He said that whenever he found himself in an unfamiliar part of town or a new city he always knew exactly where to eat thanks to one tell-tale sign. "The windows," he revealed with a grin. If they've been scrubbed, he said, he'd bet his beansprouts that the fridge was preened and the cooker was gleaming. The little things matter.

The same goes for all workplaces – on cleanliness yes – but also on how the smallest of signals can also transmit something more meaningful about who you are and what you're up to. Your "mission" in management speak. The truth is, the spaces our firms inhabit offer clues about our priorities, preoccupations and yes, our pitfalls too. And you don't need to be a canny Sydneysider or an industry hawk to see it. The corners you've cut (or the care you've taken) can speak volumes.

Traditional offices – the bigger ones anyway – were the direct descendants of factories and all the more joyless for it. You clocked in, did a specific job to the rhythm and tick of the clock and then you left. They were arranged hierarchically (corner offices for the big wigs, mahogany desks for the managers, little to delight in for the drones). These churches to commerce were built for efficiency. Picture the lines of neatly arrayed desks loaded with clattering typewriters and the rustle of paperwork – line-managers up front ever-watchful like stern invigilators in an echoey exam hall.

From the 1960s, partitions arrived to offer some nod towards privacy and personalisation (and perhaps more pragmatically, soundproofing given the rise in desktop phones). As we scoot through the decades we saw the advent of the wheely chair, the arrival of the computer and the death knell of clocking in as we knew it (much to the chagrin of those of us who now need to be constantly "on" and keep our phones, and on them our emails, within arm's reach as we sleep). The arrival of the internet, then wireless devices promised freedom from our desks to work, say from a beach in Cancún or a cabin in the Adirondacks, but somehow this mirage never fully materialised. Homeworking all the time simply doesn't work for most people.

A decent office in a friendly part of town is useful for clients, customers – staying connected to the industry and investment – and tempting talent to the workforce. It's why so many technology firms (the ones who preach the importance of the internet in liberating anyone to do anything, anywhere) have found themselves crammed into the same area around Cupertino. Industries, as well as offices, thrive in specific places.

So we're agreed that we *need* some space, at least some of the time, but we're at a creative crossroads when it comes to what an office should look like. I hope that most of us agree that our workplaces shouldn't follow the factory model. Maybe also that the need for clean air, natural light, perhaps a plant or two could be nice – but beyond that there's little consensus. Some tech companies (you know the ones, with slides and ping-pong tables and running tracks next to the routers) made the mistake of thinking offices should mimic playgrounds – that staff wanted to be treated like children. Other firms feel they're making a point by being conspicuously lean – telling the story of their disruption of an industry through cutting corners and illustrating their thriftiness through found furniture, plain walls and a few ironic posters. Then there's the more-money-than-sense crowd who have the capital in place but still splurged for tower-top, chrome-trimmed opulence.

So find a middle ground and think carefully about what your office says about you. Invest in spaces that reward those who work there and visit. Use natural materials and think about investing in and commissioning local furniture studios, architects and nearby businesses in the fit-out to show your commitment to the 'hood. Oh, and clean the windows now and again. Remember, a workspace that represents your values (as well as your value) represents a good deal indeed.

HITTING THE MARK
How to find your brand
by Brian Collins

The expert: Collins is the founder of his eponymous design studio.

The lesson: What comes before the design of your brand? Company values. Work out what they are and stick to them. If all goes well, no one will know that your first employee was *technically* your mum.

I started my first design company when I was 22 years old. I had no money so I worked out of the bedroom that I grew up in, set up a drafting table and ran a telephone line down the hallway and into the kitchen. My mom would answer the phone and say, "The Brian Collins Design Group". This was a conscious branding decision: I wanted to be seen as having a group of people or a company. It gave me a greater chance of landing bigger, better projects. Incredibly, it worked.

Today, I'm chief creative officer of Collins. We're an independent strategy and brand-experience design company in San Francisco and New York. We work with some of the most remarkable brands in the world, including Spotify, Nike and The San Francisco Symphony.

From the moment that you start talking about your company, launch a website or have someone answer your phone, there's a brand there. So my argument is simple: be conscious of it. Protect it. Manage it like you would any valuable asset. Today the big challenge is no longer finding new business ideas but instead building attention for them.

You create a brand by asking two key questions. First, what do you believe? That's an internal question that is about authenticity: what's the world seeking that only you can provide? Second, how do you

TOP TIP
It's never too early to ask yourself what your brand truly is – in terms of values as well as appearance

behave? How are you relevant for your customers? At the intersection of your belief and behaviour sits your brand. A good brand seamlessly connects what it says with what it does. And the brands that are thriving right now recognise that people no longer buy only what you make. They buy who, what, where, when, why and how you make it.

Entrepreneurs are so busy running the day-to-day puzzles of their companies that these kinds of conversations can be hard to conduct but they're necessary. These are some of the things we always want to know:

1. Why did you start this? What motivates you to get out of bed?
2. What problem do you solve? Why is that important?
3. What are your product's functional benefits?
4. What are your product's emotional benefits?
5. Why should someone trust any of this? What proof is there?
6. Who's your most respected adversary? How are they better?
7. Why will you not give up?

The top challenge facing any entrepreneur will be not knowing exactly what next step to take or figure out how everything fits together. A good brand will keep an entrepreneur focused and motivated. Best of all, it will help them answer the question at the heart of every entrepreneur's story: "what happens next?"

A WORD OF ADVICE
from Sarah Balmond, director at London-based architecture firm Balmond Studio

"Design can be everything from a well-considered logo through to a clean, intuitive website, streamlined services, intelligent processes and, of course, stand-out environments, interiors and architecture. Wield it in the right ways and design can be immensely powerful – above all, it's a human process, deeply linked with emotion. Integrate a design approach from the very beginning. And if things are going wrong, design can sometimes be the fix too. Revisit your business regularly and use design to steer it. Turn to common sense and intuition. Design could just be the glue sticking your entire operation together."

The power of the brand
by Alain Sylvain

The expert: Sylvain is the founder and CEO of his New York-based strategy and design consultancy of the same name. The firm provokes progress for companies, people and society at large.

The lesson: You have your name, uniform and packaging but what about your brand's actual identity. Have you thought about that? Here are a few questions to get you started.

Entrepreneurs are celebrated for their inspirational leadership, unconventional wisdom and brave ideas. But to craft an enduring company, they must first understand the power of "brand" – how the organisation's identity connects with users on an emotional level and informs business decisions.

In the 1970s, a young industrial designer from a small town was growing increasingly frustrated with the state of the vacuum cleaner. After seeing how a local saw mill worked, he was inspired and began experimenting with how he could shrink the concept down. Over the next 15 years he committed himself to bringing the concept to life, building 5,127 prototypes along the way.

That designer was James Dyson – and today, Dyson is an iconic brand. Not only did he fill an untapped need, but today it continues to be deeply aligned with a consumer base that values intuitiveness, aesthetics, functionality and reliability.

Ironically, James Dyson has been quoted as saying that "branding" is ignored entirely within his company. But in fact, he clearly has a better understanding of the concept than most. So what are the main questions to ask when finding your brand?

1. **Why does your company exist?**
Great brands are founded on more than just an idea for a product or service. At their core, these brands have unearthed a purpose that transcends any one thing they provide, and addresses the ultimate reason they exist at all. From the moment your idea strikes, an obsession with fulfilling it should be evident in every move you make.

2. **What does your brand mean to your audience?**
Above all else, understand your audience – who they are and what they need, so that you can build a proposition that successfully delivers on it. The modern consumer is complex, and the disposable nature of culture today means that needs and wants are ever-changing.

3. **How does your brand manifest itself?**
Once the reason for your firm's existence is established it's time to create discipline and architecture around how you manifest it all. It should include guardrails around things like tonality, values, actions in-the-now and long-term commitments, spanning the products, services, communication and experiences you provide. More importantly, emphasis should be placed on how to use these tools in a way that imbues them with timeless relevance, to account for future changes to technology and our culture-at-large.

> **TOP TIP**
> Identity is a complex and powerful concept: it's not just about repetition, it's about soul

A WORD OF ADVICE
from Dr Peter de Boer, co-founder of Amsterdam-based craft beer business Willsark

"Reframing is a very useful tool when it comes to re-evaluating your brand identity. If your company's one practical value, for instance, is being attentive then go through all the steps of your customer journey and ask yourself, 'Is this attentive for my customers?' A way to visualise this is to imagine that someone like Richard Branson walks into your office. What will he change? Try and reframe everything with Virgin in mind. You can do the same exercise with a number of different brands – from Apple to MONOCLE. Imagine what these companies would change about yours and I guarantee that you will get new ideas."

Ask the experts —— Brand identity

025

The importance of provenance
by Shamil Thakrar

The expert: Thakrar co-founded Dishoom in 2010 and continues to lead the business, which has eight restaurants and more than 1,000 team members. He believes that for something to succeed, it must have a little poetry to it.

The lesson: Food is a universal obsession and every dish has a story to tell, so make sure to do so authentically – it might just make that treat a little more tasty.

I've been a proud Londoner for decades. Living here, it's easy to take for granted the many cultures and traditions that jostle happily against each other. If you are hungry, without giving it too much thought you might easily eat Antipodean breakfast, Cantonese lunch, English afternoon tea and Indian supper. You could continue for some time without repeating a cuisine. If you select your restaurants thoughtfully, each meal would be a special one.

No doubt this is all delicious and consuming food is its own sincere joy. However, there is surely extra pleasure to be had if we pause between mouthfuls and consider (even lightly) the social and cultural context. It is a delightful thought that our meal might only be the very top layer, the culmination of generations of cooking, recipes or techniques devotedly handed down.

It feels lovely and human to know that someone first dreamt up a recipe or a dish, say, to feed Bombay's textile workers. That yesterday's vegetables were first mashed up, cooked and doused with butter perhaps a hundred years ago and served with buns, themselves with Portuguese

ancestry, for convenience and nutrition. This dish – *pau bhaji* – is one of Bombay's most dear staples that is served with love by street vendors, most deliciously where the Arabian Sea laps up against Bombay's famous beach, Girgaon Chowpatty.

Then consider the memories that so many have of devouring *pau bhaji* there in the warm breeze, watching the golden sunset across the bay, the children nearby playing cricket in the sand. When you eat the dish, you are not just tasting its combined ingredients. You are tasting the culmination of its history and the poetry that it carries with it. The dish and its context are inseparable. They are one.

Of course, then, the inevitable question: what does a restaurateur do with this? How do you respect this, stay true to this? These are questions I've been worrying about since 2010 when we opened Dishoom's first restaurant. Knowing where your food – or rather product – is from is something we all need to consider. If you are cooking a cuisine, it is worth understanding it deeply beyond recipe and technique. At a historical, even poetical level. In fact, the provenance of your product – no matter what your business – is crucial. When you have found it, the loveliness and the romance of it, you must respect it, be grateful to it and perhaps if you are lucky you will fall in love with it.

Then, naïve as this may sound, express this love. As restaurateurs, we can cook the most delicious version of a dish we can manage. And we can tell you a little about what you are eating on a small menu or in a short interaction. We can take people from our team to Bombay every year. We can tell stories through design. We can write books of recipes and history. At Dishoom, we've tried to do all of this, perhaps obsessively. And it is my strong (and perhaps romantic) belief that doing all of this, being true and authentic to the dish, will make it that touch more tasty.

The secret to looking the part
by Robert Bound

The expert: A founding editor of MONOCLE and the presenter of *Monocle on Culture* on Monocle24, Bound's favourite uniform is the unofficial one of 1970s reportage photographers such as Don McCullin.

The lesson: While making your staff wear a fussy outfit might seem great at the time, the overall impression of a job well done is far more important. So when you're sizing up a fancy epaulette or wondering about suits and skirts, the golden rule of uniforms abides: would you wear it, boss?

Everyone's favourite scene in *Catch Me If You Can*, Steven Spielberg's zippy ride through the life and crimes of the 1970s conman Frank Abagnale Jr, is when our man (played with a twinkle by Leonardo di Caprio) fakes his pilot licence and as "Captain Abagnale" escorts a 747's-worth of Pan-Am air stewardesses on a promotional tour of Europe. Sinatra belts out "Come Fly With Me" as Di Caprio becomes the grinning filling in a toothsome baby-blue sandwich. Sure, the chutzpah's to be saluted, but it's those uniforms – from the pencil-skirts to the pillbox hats – that swung it.

How come? Well, uniforms are designed to send a signal but the supposed sexiness of Pan-Am's is a projection from a more permissive era. In fact, the structured jackets and knee-length skirts advertises a certain sobriety, smartness and service

– perhaps it's the very idea of restraint that's stirring some sweet mischief beneath the surface?

A uniform should signal the attributes of the brand and the expertise of its staff. The tough brown workwear of the UPS delivery driver broadcasts an unfussy ability to get the parcel there on time; at its best the smart utilitarianism of most traditional police uniforms signals a civic rather than martial strength; the waiter in his salt-and-pepper get-up practically tells the diner what's for dinner – that they're in a brasserie, appetite whetted for the inevitable *steak-frites*.

Meanwhile, the well-drilled forecourt staff at South Korean service stations are a joy to behold – a blur of washing, buffing, oil, water and tyre-checking faultlessness – all carried out by smiling young dudes in pressed and pristine logo'd overalls (and you thought K-Pop videos had sharp choreography). The uniform, again, is a powerful brand shorthand.

Smart packaging – it's all in the design
by Verònica Fuerte

The expert: The founder of Barcelona-based creative studio Hey, Fuerte is adept at all things design – here she tackles perfect packaging.

The lesson: There's plenty to be said for the power of a well-designed jar, tin, box or bottle to get your brand out there but creating packaging that pops isn't easy. So how can you help get your product on – and off – the shelf?

Why is the design of packaging so important?
Packaging is the identity – and face – of a brand applied to a product. It's arguably as important as the product itself because it is the first contact a consumer will have with your company. Therefore it needs to be both appealing and also faithfully represent the product within.

What do you need to consider?
Branding is fundamental to creating a successful product. It all starts with considering the basics: what typeface should you use? What is the visual language? What colour should you choose? Then there's sustainability: what paper, materials and inks should represent your firm? As designers we are also responsible for these choices.

Are there any golden rules?
As with all branding projects the aim is to represent the identity of the company with the best visual language. The world of packaging design is incredibly competitive so you will need to be unique and stand out from the competition. In my opinion businesses should be open to taking risks as that is often the only way to be truly unique.

Is there anything that existing companies should think about when rebranding?
Consider what is already working when it comes to your packaging – there's no need to start from scratch if some elements are still a success. Instead, brands should focus on what isn't working so well and go from there. Designers often want to change everything when they are designing something but it's important to keep a sense of what already works for you and your brand.

Ask the experts —— Brand identity

1. Branded stationery

2. Matching glassware

3. Plants

4. A library

5. A well-stocked fridge

6. Breakfast

7. Cosy corners

Why details matter
by Hester Underhill

The expert: Underhill is the assistant editor on MONOCLE's books team – and a keen advocate for cracking open a beer with colleagues at the end of the week.

The lesson: How do you create a working environment that's both fit for purpose and a joy to occupy? It's the little things that can make all the difference.

1. **Branded stationery**
   Investing in quality notecards, labels and writing paper is never money wasted, so go for the best paper stock you can afford. Well-designed company notebooks are also a good signifier that you're running a slick operation.
2. **Matching glassware**
   Make sure you've got a uniform selection of smart drinking vessels to neaten up desks. We're sure you *are* the world's best Dad but perhaps the mug should stay at home.
3. **Plants**
   Not only do they look good but studies have shown that employees are significantly more productive when surrounded by office plants. Just looking at greenery is supposedly an effective stress reliever.
4. **A library**
   Sometimes it helps to get away from screens to find inspiration. Having an array of titles you can turn to for ideas may sound anachronistic but the internet doesn't always have the answers.
5. **A well-stocked fridge**
   Whether it's a cold bottle of sparkling water to offer guests in a business meeting or a few frosty ones for Friday drinks, it pays to have a liberal stash of libations on hand.
6. **Breakfast**
   Providing breakfast is an effective way of bringing together colleagues across departments. There's nothing like breaking bread when it comes to creating a sense of community and fostering friendships within a business.
7. **Cosy corners**
   Open-plan spaces might be the norm today but make sure you have a few quiet spots where people can get a sense of respite from the office buzz and properly focus in peace.

Ask the experts —— Brand identity

029

3.
Funding

You're off the mark, now you need the cash – but how do you source it? And once you've got it, how do you keep your company's finances afloat?

BANK ON IT
A guide to getting funding
by Pip Jamieson

The expert: Jamieson is founder and CEO of The Dots, a professional networking site for the creative industries.

The lesson: Convincing others to back your concept is a vital step in getting an idea off the drawing board or scaling up a nascent business. Here's how to go about finding investors.

I had to build my network from scratch. I had meeting after meeting, slowly working my way up the ladder. My break came when someone introduced me to Brent Hoberman, co-founder of Lastminute.com. He loved what we were doing and introduced me to a number of my seed investors.

The goal of my company, The Dots, is to take on LinkedIn, which was built for traditional, corporate careers. I wanted to create an alternative professional solution, with a modern workforce in mind. Our early adopters worked in the creative economy, but the network expanded rapidly and we're now home to an ever-expanding list of inclusive and values-driven professional communities. Today we have nearly one million members, and I'm on a 10-year journey to become the biggest professional network.

I had the luxury of selling my previous business and seed-investing The Dots myself when it launched in 2014. Since then, we've completed two rounds of funding, raising €1.7m in the first external round and €4m in the second. But just because I've approached venture capitalists (VCs), it doesn't mean that it's right for you and your business. The first thing you have to ask yourself is whether you want to take on that money, because

the moment you do, you are not in control of your company anymore. You have other people who you are accountable to.

My advice is to make sure you research all available avenues. If you're going down a route like mine, realise that many VCs either want a billion-dollar business or they don't care if you go under. That's the journey I have chosen – I've made this my whole life – but it's not right for everyone. Sometimes, a loan or grant is the best way to get you off the ground, and there are numerous options out there. Angel investment (wealthy individuals known as "angels" who back businesses) is another avenue, particularly in the UK where they get tax breaks.

What I'm also increasingly interested in is crowdfunding with the likes of Seedrs or Crowdcube. I love the idea of raising part of the money from my community and having them benefit from any growth. If I could be fully accountable to my community and not shareholders, that would be my dream. But I'd want to make sure that there's a sensible cap so that no one's putting in more money than they can afford to lose, because every business is risky.

If you do go down the "angel" or VC route, it's about picking your investors carefully and making sure they align with your values. I love the diversity of my backers, whom I call shareholders (it gives you the sense that you're all in the same boat) but communication is key for maintaining these relationships. We regularly send updates to them, in which we are very honest about the things that are going right and the things that are going wrong. Involving the shareholders on the journey is important, particularly as you may need them to reinvest in the future. We're always open to asking for help too – my shareholders have been an incredible source of client introductions – but be sure to push back if they overstep the mark. When pitching for investment, I'd also highly recommend spending the first few weeks getting in some practise runs and pitching to investors you're not that interested in. Some of my best mentors are investors who have turned me down. They now help with different areas of my business, from tech to scaling. Don't get upset when you get a no. If you like an investor, keep in touch and ask their advice when you need it. They might have turned you down in the last round, but they might invest next time.

Recently we've been inundated with people wanting to invest in The Dots, which is a really lovely position to be in, but it takes time for you to get on investors' radars. You've got to be patient. Focus on building a brilliant product and it does happen, I promise, it just takes a while.

My top tips for securing funding:

1. Create an outstanding pitch deck.
2. Build a network as early as possible. Investors, particularly VCs, build relationships with founders for years before investing.
3. Build a portfolio of mentors. I can turn to mine for advice and having that knowledge base is incredibly valuable.
4. Get advice from fellow founders who have been there and done that.
5. Persevere. Every no leads to a yes – I'm living proof. If I can do it, anyone can.
6. Choose your investors wisely.
7. Don't do it because everyone else is doing it, only raise funds if you have to.

It's all in the budget: how to create yours
by Josie Baker

The expert: Baker is the co-founder of Holt Baker, a legal and finance consultancy firm.

The lesson: When it comes to creating your business plan, the budget is an important tool and it's vital you get it right. It should provide a financial road map but it can also help drive the brand, make decisions and focus on long-term goals.

So, what is a budget?
It includes a profit and loss account, a balance sheet and cashflow – they all depend on one another and each provides a different financial measure. The profit and loss account, for instance, sets out a company's revenues, expenses and profits from the operating activity, or "trade", during a stated period (usually 12 months). The balance sheet reports a company's assets, liabilities (at the top) and shareholders' equity (at the bottom). It provides a snapshot of the company's assets at a given point in time. The top and bottom must equal, hence the name "balance sheet". And a cashflow shows physical cash inflows and outflows from trade, investing and financing activities over a stated period, which is usually 12 months.

And its purpose?
1. To set out the operating activity you intend to achieve.
2. To demonstrate how you intend to realise future success. This is useful when pitching to investors.
3. To show a timeline of what resources will be needed and when.

How do you prepare one?
Building a budget is not easy; it takes research, consideration and revision. Always keep in mind the purpose and only include what you believe can be achieved in the time period.

The first step is to research assumptions for the period ahead. These are based on your past performance, target market and appropriate speculation.

Start with revenue, cost of goods sold and gross margin, then selling, general and administrative expenses. Further assumptions will be required for capital expenditure and working capital terms. Finally, you need assumptions for any funding that you expect to receive.

Next prepare your three financial statements: profit and loss, balance sheet and cashflow. Once complete, take time away. If anything doesn't make sense, edit and adjust. If there are still elements you are not sure of, don't be afraid to ask an accountant or finance consultant. Getting your budget right is essential to maximising your business's chance of success.

What should you consider when creating yours?
1. Make sure it's robust. Build your budget using solid assumptions that will stand up to scrutiny.
2. Be realistic. It should be a representation of what you believe will happen in your business's future.
3. Review. The budget is a working tool for now and the future. It should be regularly reviewed to ensure it is robust and realistic.

WORTHY INVESTMENT

How to put together the perfect pitch

by Marie Perruchet

The expert: Amsterdam-based Perruchet is an international marketing and communications director who has worked with the likes of Netflix, LinkedIn and Adidas.

The lesson: This is your chance to grab an investor's attention – show them that you are innovative and that your idea is going to make the world a better place in one way or another.

I lived in Silicon Valley for 10 years and became accustomed to seeing 10 entrepreneurs pitch the same idea in the same hour. I soon realised that storytelling is essential. As a former journalist I know how to make people talk, gain their trust and tell their story but, from my experience, that is not always the case with entrepreneurs. To simplify your story into a five-minute pitch takes a lot of work and practice. The process is important but never forget what you want to achieve. Aim for fluency while keeping these universal rules in mind:

1. **Keep it short**
   Don't wait five minutes to dive into it and don't beat around the bush. Take the first 10 seconds to grab your audience's attention.
2. **Be clear and precise**
   Make every word count. You can paint pictures in your listener's mind to help them remember your idea.
3. **Be authentic**
   You don't want to sound like a clone of yourself. People want to see the real person behind the venture.

4. **Research your audience and know who you're addressing**
   Perhaps there is something that could help you forge a connection.
5. **Test your pitch in front of a low-stakes audience such as a group of friends**
   Ask your audience to reformulate your pitch to see what they understood and took away from it. Practise will help you gain confidence and when the day comes for you to pitch your business to an investor, you'll be ready. I would recommend recording your pitch so that you can listen to yourself and make the necessary improvements.
6. **Go with the flow – don't script it**
   You don't want your pitch to sound too rehearsed or robotic. It's like driving: when you first start learning you're so tense that everyone's afraid to sit next to you, but with some practise you relax and start holding conversations and doing all sorts of things that you probably shouldn't while driving. When you're pitching you should feel just as confident and relaxed.
7. **Get the timing right**
   I always prefer to pitch on mid-week mornings. That's because people are catching up with their emails on Mondays and they're distracted by thinking about the upcoming weekend on Fridays.
8. **Repetition is no bad thing**
   We've all watched politicians and how they tend to deliver their top three messages regardless of the questions they're asked. Figure out what you want to get out of the meeting and what three messages you want to get across. Make sure your top messages are conveyed and repeated so that they sink in.

I crowdfunded my business, here's why you should too
by Phil Ellis

The expert: Ellis is the co-founder of Beryl (previously Blaze), which manufactures bike lights and operates a bike-rental scheme in a number of cities. It was also an early adopter of this funding option.

The lesson: Essentially asking lots of people for a small amount of money, crowdfunding is a viable choice for many. Let us walk you through three routes to consider.

1. **Equity**
   Investors receive shares in return for investments and will be inextricably linked to your business as they own a part of the company. The cash generated is pretty much free to be spent by the business in whatever way they think is most appropriate and will help to build up a potential network of advocates, advisors and supporters all with "skin in the game". However, you now have many more shareholders to whom you owe fiduciary duties, and with future financing it is difficult to predict if they will "follow-on" for more fundraising.

2. **Rewards**
   For this option, rewards are given in return for donations. Blaze offered contributors the first products we made, which gave us early product validation. With this avenue, you get a big bunch of early adopters who you can choose to work with to make improvements to your products. However, the majority of the money you raise will go straight into creating the product rather than other things that help to grow the business, like sales teams.

3. **Debt**
   A lot of the financial crowdfunding platforms also offer debt funding, usually in the form of a corporate bond. You'll need to be a bigger business and definitely generate revenues for this option, maybe even be profitable. A corporate bond is pure debt. It won't impact the shareholding of the business but now you owe somebody money and you have to meet the re-payments. Compared to a normal bond you can probably get a better price (lower interest) and you'll get all the benefits of a big engaged group of investors.

So what's right for your business? If you want to grow quickly and are looking at crowdfunding because you don't like the idea of going to VCs or angel investors, then equity is a great option. However, if you've got a great product you want to have some fun with then the rewards model could work for you.

Make sure you get everything in order before you launch – have answers prepared for the most likely questions and be ready to engage with the crowd during the process. The first 24 hours are very important. Only launch your campaign when you can be certain that at least the first 25 per cent of the requirement is already committed behind the scenes. You should be able to individually name who is going to invest in the first 24 hours and the amount will make up at least 25 per cent of the total goal.

TOP TIP
Crowdfunding may be an exciting way to inject some cash but remember, it's not without accountability

A WORD OF ADVICE
from Max Dautresme, co-founder of Hong Kong design agency Substance

"Doing business with friends, so the wisdom goes, is neither advisable nor likely to result in a successful outcome. When searching for investors, many look to big names but in my experience the best opportunities can often be found right before our eyes. I met my latest investor during a lunch with friends. It was a fortuitous encounter that enabled me to grow my business by 20 per cent. I connected with him because of a shared interest and a partnership grew from there. In fact, there is something to be said for choosing to work with the type of people who share your sensibilities, tastes and interests."

Ask the experts —— Funding

A WORD OF ADVICE
from Camille Kriebitzsch, the principal of Parisian venture-capital fund Eutopia

"Bringing in an investor is a bit like getting married: you don't just want their money, you want a partner to help you grow. That's why you need to know who you're asking, why you're asking them, exactly how much you need and when you're going to need it. Begin talking six months to a year before you need the money. This gives you a chance to get to know one another. It's important that they knows you as a person because that's what they're investing in: your commitment, your charisma and the strength of your vision. In the long run, the team behind a product will make or break an investment."

TOP TIP
Being the creative mind behind a business doesn't excuse you from some number-crunching – you need to go all in

ON THE MONEY
Understanding cashflow
by Ruchika Sachdeva

The expert: Sachdeva is the founder of Bodice, luxury clothing brand in Delhi that aims to take Indian fashion worldwide.

The lesson: Sure, it sounds simple – just calculate the money coming in and out – but managing cashflow is where many businesses go wrong. Make sure you aren't one of them.

While I was studying at university, we would joke about how struggling financially was a symptom of being a creative genius. By this we meant that if your creations were commercially viable then you weren't original enough. But how does one run a successful business and come up with groundbreaking designs? This was my biggest dilemma when I started my clothing label Bodice 10 years ago. Little did I know that it's the cushion of cashflow that gives you the freedom to take risks, hire great talent and experiment.

This brings us to the question: how does one ensure a regular inflow of money to survive and, more importantly, flourish? Fashion is a creative field that thrives on ideas but in the end it's still a business. My guiding principles through this journey are two-fold: data and planning. Data analysis sounded intimidating when I first started but it can be as simple as keeping a diary and observing patterns. Record information such as who is your customer, why are they buying your product and how. These simple questions can deliver invaluable insights into your business.

They say it's about finding a winning idea but success largely depends on the execution.

Educate yourself
A college degree is great but going out into the real world is a whole different story. Being an entrepreneur requires you to learn about the entire ecosystem of running a business, from managing employees to marketing and accounting. Yes, you can hire people in but it's your business and no one knows the larger vision better than you do. I am a creative director but the majority of my time goes into setting systems for different departments and improving. I have a great team but when they are stuck, it's my job to show up – and for that I need to constantly educate myself.

Do your research
Running your own business involves tackling various things simultaneously. I organise them into small projects – this helps me plan and execute better, and I always start with research. Who are the experts in the topic I am researching? Have they written any books or recorded any podcasts?

Be prepared for challenges
It's risky business being an entrepreneur, no matter how well you do your homework. Of course you should save up for rainy days and reach out for loans when needed but it's important to have a contingency plan when everything else fails. When this happens, one has to persist, find creative solutions and take tough decisions to survive. In tricky times, I reach out to my network of mentors for advice, vendors for credit and our community for support.

What are investors looking for?
by Antoine Baschiera, Jade Francine and Aurélien Drain

The experts: Antoine Baschiera is co-founder and CEO of Early Metrics, a rating agency for start-ups and small businesses; Jade Francine is co-founder and COO of We Maintain, a start-up in the elevator maintenance industry and Aurélien Drain is the head of business development for HSBC private banking.

———————————————

The lesson: A group of experts and entrepreneurs based in Paris give us their take on the topic of funding a start-up.

MONOCLE (M): Antoine, what are investors looking for when it comes to start-ups?

ANTOINE BASCHIERA (AB): The most important assets in young companies are the people starting the project. When business angels invest in the early days of a company, they tend to have a strong focus on who the founders are – not only their skills but also on their capacity to self-assess, to pivot and to challenge themselves.

JADE FRANCINE (JF): I agree – it's about people. Funding is critical when you're launching a business but actually when you have a good project, money is kind of a commodity – and it's not that hard to find. As an entrepreneur you need to find investors with a connection to your industry.

AB: You could start by listing your dream investor, someone that will add value to your business and then try and contact them.

> **TOP TIP**
> Investors will accompany you on a (hopefully) long journey so pay attention to the people behind the money

AURÉLIEN DRAIN (AD): I absolutely agree with you both. Our clients are very keen to invest in start-up businesses. They don't only look at the return on investments, they also think in terms of social impact and social responsibility. Funding is important, but we're also very keen to create good connections, good synergy and create business opportunities.

M: How important is it to do your homework when it comes to funding?

AD: There are no golden rules for raising funds or approaching investors but what we can say is that it's important to develop your vision and prove that the timing is good for your business. You need to convince your audience but it's also important to prove your capacity to execute and show that your team is behind you. Your team is absolutely crucial. An investor believes in an idea, they're investing in the people. The business plan also is important but don't be too worried about the figures because any investor knows that these are always wrong in terms of prediction, especially for start-ups. It's more important to focus on when the breakeven points could be and cashflow.

M: Jade, tell us how did you decide the timing was right for you.

JF: There were a few criteria to hit before we approached funding – the team, technology, conversions. But it was also about myself as the founder. You have to ask yourself, do you feel ready to go and pitch to people?

AB: There are good and bad times to approach investors. For instance, do you need that money to get to the next milestone? If you're close to achieving your first sale or expanding into a new country, don't raise money. You need to do so just after you've reached a milestone.

JF: When it came to choosing our investors, we opted for people who share our values and ambitions. In the end, these are people you see every six weeks.

AD: Yes, absolutely. The fit is very important because it's a long-term relationship, it's not just about money. It's about reporting, offering transparency and having regular contact with them. You need to be in a very trusted environment with your investors.

4.
Community

Bringing people together – whether that's within your team, connecting with other businesses in the area or even fostering a global network of loyal supporters – will be one of your company's biggest strengths, so it's something worth investing in.

BETTER TOGETHER

How to nurture a good company culture
by Kate Marlow

The expert: Kate Marlow is the co-founder of Here Design, a multidisciplinary creative studio.

The lesson: There's more to feeling part of a tight-knit team than daily meetings and coffee breaks. Branch out and encourage your colleagues to engage with one another.

One of my favourite Vivienne Westwood slogans reads, "You get out what you put in". And you know what? She's right. Today's society is on the edge of a cultural abyss – we have become mundane and what we put in is having a negative effect on what we could get out. Here Design believes in the richness of culture in its creative output but also in the studio ethos. Enriching the experience for those who are part of Here has always been integral to the journey. Here's how we do it:

1. **Cultivate your community**
   We cook and eat together every Friday around a communal table. It is natural for people to connect over food and bringing this into the workplace offers a moment to nourish bodies and minds together through shared conversation and knowledge. The community you create between your team is your halo – and remember, it can also be perceived by those on the outside. Team unity will be felt by your clients and industry peers; it's crucial for carving out your company's space within the world.

2. **Celebrate and nurture**
   The best way to foster company culture is to celebrate the people you work with through experiences that add value to work life while also being creatively liberating. Underpinning our studio experience is what we have called the "Here Year". All activities we do together follow the natural seasons: spring, summer, autumn and winter. In spring we celebrate newness, in summer we enjoy liberation, in autumn we take stock and order and in winter we focus on unity. Find a model that is relevant to your business but ensure it offers an opportunity to sit back, reflect and enjoy working together.

3. **Real life encounters lead the way**
   Over the years, we've seen the development of Microsoft Teams, Slack and other similar internal communication resources. We've often thought about elevating this idea of sharing in the workplace – how can we share the rich talent, imagination and skills our team possess just as easily? So we created our own almanac to serve as a cultural programme of learning – it aims to articulate the work we do. Each season, a core group chosen from varying disciplines create and develop a seven week-long programme which explores a theme in depth. We keep this away from client work; with the content being created for and presented to the studio only.

   We also have our radio show, Hear Here. The show is a culmination of the previous week's highlights, where we share ideas, interviews, thoughts and DJ sets. This sharing of our own creativity exists in a multi-dimensional way, from the almanac and radio show, to the kitchen we eat in and the physical office we sit in. Be creative with what you have and focus on using real-life encounters to nurture growth.

Engaging with the global community
by Oooota Sebastian Adepo

The expert: Adepo is the founder of Dynein and Cross Culture Creative, platforms she uses respectively to recognise global hospitality and facilitate investment in Africa.

The lesson: While it's tempting to reach out to those you know for help, it could be beneficial to ask new communities for a fresh perspective. Open up the conversation, you never know what you might get in return.

The word community is defined as either a group of individuals living together within a larger society or those who share common interests and characteristics. The former has categorised us for millennia; today we are increasingly determining ourselves by the latter. But why is this? It is mostly because of modern-day technology which allows individuals to form bonds with those of similar values, views and preferences. Rather than searching the local pool of people, they are able to discover their individual identity – as well as a group that they belong to. But to what extent does this transform our possibilities in work and life, particularly in a globalised world?

Communities are like snowflakes – unique and in constant formation. And there seems to be one for almost everyone. While many groups can feel inaccessible due to their principles, their code of behaviour and sometimes their need for protection, a global community is based on openness. It forsakes borders, religion, and ethnicity in favour of fraternity – and it seeks nothing more than willing participants. In fact, conversing with people in different cities, countries or even continents can help blur this distinction between physical connectedness and common interests.

In our personal lives, we can expand our sense of belonging and reap its rewards by consciously choosing activities outside our routines and social bubbles. Networking, either in person, online or through a group of people you trust is fine but perhaps attend an event with those whose interests you know nothing about. I always revert to my childhood curiosities, things I excelled at but never had a chance

TOP TIP
Who says that proximity is a prerequisite for a successful network? Broaden your horizons

to pursue, as well as those I never gave myself a chance to be good at. With the internet constantly reinforcing our silos, we need to seek out these opportunities, meet new people and discover fresh points of view.

The same is true when it comes to business. In fact, diverse ideas are crucial to driving innovation – recruiting talent without fully understanding this can undercut the potential of a team or organisation. Diverse faces and perspectives within your team are as important as it is to actively engage with businesses in other parts of the world. And doing so can lead to untraditional yet effective results. A US-based company that specialises in supply chain management with a specific regional focus could benefit from building relationships with a Turkish or Kenyan company in the same field. Sure, their ways of operating may vary but the sharing of ideas could be unexpectedly informative. It may simply bring about an understanding of suppliers and operating conditions in a different area, or it may lead to partnerships, mentorships and mergers that feel organic.

Ultimately though we are social creatures with habits that determine the communities we form. From childhood, we're wired to associate them with the familiar. But if we want to take advantage of friendships and partnerships that could add great value to our lives, we need to actively seek interests and attitudes that differ from what we know. There will always be grey areas and we probably won't agree with everyone's views and patterns of behaviour. At the very least, we will become better listeners. More likely than not, we will emerge with a broadened sense of possibility.

POWER TO THE PEOPLE

Forging a loyal community – and how to do it

by Rob Smith

The expert: Hailing from the west coast of Canada, Rob grew up surfing, skiing and running. He blended these passions with his love of design in Vancouver Running Co, which he founded with his wife Becky in 2015.

The lesson: Take time to nurture your company's supporters and make them feel a part of something. Not only will it enrich your brand but it makes good business sense too.

Community by its very nature is a rather ambiguous word, laden in subjectivity and applied in any number of ways. Is it the physical space your business occupies? Is it the neighbourhood that you've made your base? Or is it the people that live in the cities and towns in which we choose to lay our roots? It is in fact all of them but most significantly it embodies who you are at the core of your company, the character of the team and how you outwardly show up for those who identify with your brand. Simply put, if your business were a human being, the people would be the beating heart and its community the personality.

So in that case, how do you let your character shine? How do you get it out there in a tangible way for people to experience, and better yet, become a part of? You first need to consciously separate community and revenue. If you go into this thinking you will cultivate a group of loyal supporters to generate revenue then put the pen down and back away, I'm afraid you've missed the point. Today's consumers are more educated than ever, so don't use it to sell: it will become an exercise in futility and people will see right through it.

The second point to understand is that it takes consistency to establish a strong community – much like growing a business. Remember, these are your most loyal followers and they could become your most reliable contributors. And you have to show up for them again and again to develop a presence. This process should begin on day one through a number of actions, from instore get-togethers and charitable initiatives to team away-days and digital content.

One of the best ways to engage with people though is through events. I own a running business which means we have a relatively obvious outlet to do this: our free weekly runs. These simple jogs have grown into charity races, surprise shoe deliveries, epic helicopter rides and more. But what if you're a bakery in Zermatt or a boutique financial firm in Florence, then what? How about a bi-weekly bakers' hike, where anyone who wants to join embarks on a one-hour trek followed by a pastry-making class. Or perhaps a monthly "grapes of cash" gathering where locals meet and discuss aspects of managing personal wealth followed by lessons pertaining to wines of the Chianti region.

When appropriate, follow up with a personal account of these events – a simple email or social media post will help make your clients feel like they're included in something bigger. By nature, humans want to be a part of a group and many enjoy seeing themselves represented within one – so take advantage of this and ask those in attendance to contribute and speak positively about their experience with your brand. It will help draw in more people.

Granted, cultivating your community can be emotionally draining at times. There will be days when you want nothing more than to crawl under a rug, hugging a bottle of whisky after a day of entrepreneurial battles. The last thing you will want to do is show up for that event, talk or run. On these occasions, ask for help from volunteers and staff. I guarantee they'll step up, because they too believe in you and your brand.

After all your hard work, there will eventually come a point when your commitment manifests into something beautiful, something that truly represents the personality of your brand. And as long as you are open to listening and learning, it will help guide you and inform your business and teach you things you never thought possible. You will have the opportunity to relax and let others take the helm, and when things gain momentum, it will even begin perpetuating itself. Community has the power to change lives and those who are part of it become evangelists, spreading the gospel of your brand and vision throughout their circles, hungry for the next time they can all be together in celebration of what you've created.

A WORD OF ADVICE
from Brunello Cucinelli, founder of the eponymous Italian fashion brand

"My big theme is humane sustainability, which starts with good food for all staff. We make our own olive oil, our own wine, we grow vegetables and Senatore Cappelli wheat. I want to maintain things of great quality – not just the clothing we make, but the Italian culture of authentic cuisine, which you will find in our canteen. Just eating fresh bread and olive oil, you know that God exists. I want everyone here to be able to share that feeling. Workers and guests eat together in our canteen. The communal meal is an experience that rejuvenates human beings. I call it humane sustainability, but it should just be called normalcy."

TOP OF THE PUPS
Why every office needs a dog
by Genevieve Bates

The expert: When not occupied with the care of her Japanese shiba inu puppy, Bates serves as MONOCLE's deputy chief sub editor and chief sub editor of its sister title, *Konfekt*.

The lesson: Often spotted napping under desks, searching for snacks or getting belly rubs, pooches are the perfect addition to any office – and they're a certified morale booster too.

A fairly basic starting point for a productive office is that its occupants want to be there. If they're convivial and feel connected to those around them, even better. So how to make your office happier?

Here are some clues: it has four legs but it's not a ping-pong table. It likes to run but it's not a lunchtime personal trainer. It can be competitive but it's not a company golf tournament. It has a bark but it's not a potted tree. Yes, the shortcut to workplace contentment is to bring in a canine consultant.

Daphne, my Japanese shiba inu puppy, first came to work with me the day after Americans voted in their 2020 presidential election. It was a long, tense week at MONOCLE as we followed polls which hung by a thread, and edited our next issue, which was due to be printed before the result would be confirmed. It was also the first day of the UK's second coronavirus lockdown and there was talk of cancelling Christmas. Daphne was the delightful distraction we didn't know we'd needed.

Before Daphne became part of my working life, I'd often felt out of step with colleagues. I wonder if it was because I married and had children at a relatively young age – or if I'd have found the forced confinement and superficial jollity of office life awkward anyway. Having a dog as my constant companion fixed that. Distant officemates to whom I'd never spoken now swing by my desk to cuddle or play with Daphne. While there, they open up about their childhood pets, the dog-shaped holes in their lives and the breeds they dream of owning one day. Dogs help us to relate to each other as individuals, not merely as embodiments of our job titles. Having a pooch among your professionals is also an excellent icebreaker with visitors, job candidates and clients.

It helps that Daphne is, on any objective view, adorable, as well as quiet and fastidiously cat-like in her cleanliness – watching her clean her ears is a masterclass in resourcefulness and dexterity. But beyond my anecdotal evidence of Daphne's power to bolster morale chez MONOCLE, research *paws*-itively proves that interacting with a dog lowers stress levels and improves the functioning of our immune systems.

Because humans evolved solving problems about animals, animals have the power to focus our attention. According to a University of Pennsylvania study, "When we are around animals, we become more joyous, communicative, expressive and calm." Last but not leashed, another explanation of our affinity is that as dogs became domesticated they found that they could get what they wanted by imitating human expressions so they've evolved to be in tune with our moods. Lucky us.

Making your presence felt
by David Sax

The expert: Sax is a journalist based in Toronto. He is also the author of several books, including *The Revenge of Analog* and *The Soul of an Entrepreneur.*

The lesson: The business that knows its place as a part of the neighbourhood will be rewarded by the custom of the community.

I recently took a walk with my family along College Street, a major thoroughfare just a block from my house in Toronto. One stretch houses all sorts of businesses – grocery and clothing shops, a library, lots of restaurants, bakeries and pizzerias that together make up the western end of the city's original Little Italy.

After a year of hardships, the toll on the high street was obvious and many shopfronts remained empty. However, during our walk I was struck by hopeful signs as we passed a handful of new businesses. One of them, a Caribbean/Chinese fusion restaurant that had opened in the depths of winter, had set up a table on the pavement. There the two owners stood, handing out tea samples.

"Hi there, dear!" one of the owners called out to my seven-year-old daughter. "Do you want to try some hibiscus tea?" That offer, which of course we couldn't refuse (marketing tip: children are the soft underbelly of consumerism, even if they spit out your tea), led to a conversation with the owners about their restaurant, its menu and their background. We told them that we lived nearby and they wondered whether we'd like to try their food sometime (we would). The whole interaction lasted two minutes but it illuminated a deeper truth about entrepreneurship.

Owning a business might be an economic activity but it's built on relationships that are strongest when they are tangible and firmly rooted in the spaces and the people who exist in the physical world. Although we might talk about the impact of digital technology on our lives, the heart and soul of running your own venture remains analogue. Every business exists in a physical place and its people. The stronger its relationship to that community, the better off it will be.

Many of the businesses around me were able to respond directly to the needs of their local market – their neighbourhood, city and region – by

quickly catering to rapidly changing needs. The entrepreneurs behind these businesses knew what this neighbourhood needed because it was theirs too. They worked here and lived here, so they could respond to the area's needs in a heartbeat, far quicker than any large company could.

In return, the residents stood beside them. People who had never shopped locally before put their money into the streets where they lived, ordering takeaways directly from restaurants rather than from delivery apps, or going through the slight inconvenience of phoning in a book order rather than clicking on an Amazon link because they witnessed – in all those empty windows bandaged in brown paper – what happened when they didn't.

The deeper truth is that all of this rested not only on the physical presence of the shops, offices and restaurants here but on the face-to-face human relationships that their presence afforded.

TOP TIP
Make an effort with the people that surround you – they're the ground your business stands on

When an entrepreneur hangs out their shop sign in a community, they do so in the hope of connecting with other humans. Although on the surface this might simply look like a desire for customers, in reality these everyday interactions between an owner and their staff, suppliers evolve into real, meaningful, humanising interactions.

The brief conversation we had on the street that weekend with the woman who owned the restaurant was more than just a pleasant sip of hibiscus tea and a glance at her menu. It was the start of a relationship between us – between business owner and customer; local restaurant and local diner; neighbour and maybe even friend – that had the potential to grow into something lasting and to endure for years. The truth for entrepreneurs is that no business is virtual. They all exist somewhere and the greater the bond that an entrepreneur can forge with the places and people around them, the better off we'll all be.

MEET AND GREET

Why face-to-face is always better
by Andrew Tuck

The expert: MONOCLE's editor in chief Tuck has been heading the magazine since its launch in 2007.

The lesson: This is your business so get out there and spread the word. No one else is going to do it for you.

When you work as a journalist, interviewing people about their extraordinary lives and experiences, you soon learn an annoying fact. Just after you have packed away the mic and placed your notebook in a pocket, your subject, released from the formality of the interview, will suddenly tell you something extraordinary. Damn.

It's why, over time, you learn about the need to put people at ease, to make the technology somehow fade from their focus, and to stop this experience feeling like a performance. And then, if you can do all that, in the dark of a studio or tucked into a restaurant banquette, hopefully the magic happens: they tell you their tale in full and don't leave the best bit for when they are saying goodbye.

This is not just a media lesson. It's a business one too – and an important one. There are many people who believe that meetings with clients and customers can now all happen with swift precision via video calls and that arranging face-to-face interactions is somehow a waste of energy. And lunch with a contact? God, two hours with someone they don't know would mess with their schedules and with their carb-free diet.

Yes, we agree, with a video call you can get the performance part; the bit dictated and framed by technology where you perform for whoever has logged in. You even

get to take precise and detailed notes and mull over data-packed Powerpoint slides. But what you don't have a chance to do is calm people, to break out of the time-allotted restraints of the electronic calendar or to have those two minutes at the restaurant coat-check when you get to hear what they really think. Serendipity does not happen on a Zoom call.

Journalism and business thrive on the face-to-face. When you take time to go and visit someone it shows commitment. When you have someone's full attention you sense in seconds how the conversation should flow for the best outcome. Freed from the screen, talk also flows along more interesting routes. And when someone knows that they can speak openly – and they are not going to be caught out by someone recording the call – they can tell you their unvarnished views, tell you their concerns and give you the best advice.

It's why MONOCLE has always valued the power of being present with our outlook on journalism and business developing some shared touchpoints – go see people, hear what they have to say. It's also why the pandemic months were often frustrating.

So, in the future, go see people. Listen to what they know. Tell your story too. Discover common ground. Break bread – and catch up over coffee. Free yourself from the starchy world of tech. And, every now and then try and think like a journalist – how would you get the best out of this moment, unearth the real story? Grinning on a video call? Or making the effort to go and see them face-to-face? I think you know the answer.

All together now: considering your neighbourhood
by Yuta Oka

The expert: Oka is the co-founder of Azumi Setoda, a hotel with an onus on community, and Insitu, a developer that aims to create destinations and neighbourhoods in collaboration with local residents. Born in Japan but raised in the US, he is now very happy in his home of Setoda.

The lesson: Being a part of the bigger picture is more than just rewarding. Connect with the local community, support neighbouring companies and encourage new ideas.

Urbanisation has its place in society; for many, it means more money, more goods and more people to empower a city to be more efficient and productive. I grew up in central Tokyo and I love the city, but I grew tired of watching my favourite hangouts get torn down and replaced with chain cafés, restaurants and convenience stores. Instead, I wanted to be a part of something bigger.

I had always envisioned finding a small countryside town on the side of a lake, in the mountains or by a calm ocean front with welcoming residents and local produce. My dream was to escape the city and become involved in a new area; I wanted to find and foster a community that would survive the forces of urbanisation.

In 2015 I discovered Setoda, a small port town on an island within Setouchi. It was here that we were introduced to Horiuchi-tei, a 140-year-old estate that originally belonged to an influential salt-farming family. Today it is Azumi Setoda, a *ryokan* (a traditional Japanese inn) that puts the community at the heart of everything.

Our first visit was in January and the weather was crisp. The calm sea was a beautiful blue and the breeze had a citrus scent thanks to the tangerine and lemon trees planted throughout the island. We took a stroll down the *shotengai* (the local high street) where more than half the shops were closed. But the place didn't feel dead; children were running around and people invited us into their shops for a cup of tea. It felt right.

We wanted Azumi to express the culture of the area and eventually draw a global crowd. Setoda had been one of the most popular travel destinations within Setouchi in the 1960s thanks to a boom in tourism. The island's population had been waiting for a resurgence but this time they wanted it to be on their terms – they wanted a "livable Setoda with a human touch". As we began to plan, design and build Azumi, we presented our ideas to the local community.

Since then, the municipality has been funding our community-driven initiative to revive Setoda; we have been running workshops with the local population to ensure their vision for the area's future is realised. We have also introduced a system to match real-estate owners with young entrepreneurs, allowing them to rent the closed shops within the *shotengai*. When we first launched the initiative, we had 10 people turn up – we now have more than 100 who participate.

Our journey began with the building of Azumi Setoda but it transformed into a kind of town planning. We have listened to the local voices and since launching the *ryokan* we have also opened Yubune, a *sento* (public bath house and sauna). We have also helped to encourage new businesses into the area, including a local tavern called Soil Setoda and Overview Coffee – an American coffee roaster that specialises in sourcing coffee from farms and that follows the principles of regenerative agriculture; it has now set up a Japanese roaster. We also have lent our design skills to lemon farmers and developed new products with them.

Today's Setoda is very different from the one we arrived at in 2015. By launching Azumi and connecting with those who were here before us, we have created a place that is far more desirable for us all – tourists, business owners and residents alike. We hope that the journey will continue.

Ask the experts —— Community

TOP TIP
Success is incremental: if you lift other businesses up with you, everybody stands to benefit

The golden rules of customer service
by Sophie Grove

The expert: Grove is the editor of MONOCLE's sister publication *Konfekt*.

The lesson: No matter what you do, most jobs are in some sense customer facing. Getting it right is partly about brand building but it's also about telling your story and making the right impression – from the shine of your shoes to the tone of your emails.

1. **Curb your enthusiasm**
   Customer service is about putting people at ease, not bowling them over with your bounteous knowledge. If in doubt, err on the side of formal. Start off with eye contact and a handshake before you go in for bear hugs and high fives (if ever).

2. **Presentation matters**
   In person, this means dressing the part –ideally in an outfit that can transition from boardroom to boarding lounge, retail floor to work drinks. A well-cut uniform works for shop staff and a Boglioli blazer and Alden brogues for the CMO.

3. **The customer is sometimes wrong**
   Don't be afraid to stand up to unreasonable demands and rudeness. Be firm and fair when confronted with red-faced rabble rousers who are getting angry over something beyond your control.

4. **Hire judiciously**
   Seek out people who buy into your brand and go beyond what's expected of them. If you wouldn't fancy going for lunch with them there's a good chance your customers won't take to them either.

5. **Reward loyalty**
   If you've got them – keep them. There's no substitute for a band of truly happy, committed staff. Conversely, vexed employees will make customers feel uneasy and are less likely to go that extra mile.

6. **Lead by example**
   It's difficult to expect your staff to be fair, courteous, punctual and upbeat when their boss hits the roof at the slightest provocation. Every hire should feel valued, listened to and rewarded – they will likely apply these values to their customer service. There's nothing more compelling than an inspiring leader.

7. **Don't be afraid to sell**
   While people need space to reflect and ponder, aloof nonchalance can come across as rude. Encourage staff to open up, engage and don't be afraid to remind them they're there to make money and meet margins. It's worth remembering that some customers want to be convinced.

8. **Be a social linchpin**
   Cultivate a loyal band of "supporters" with good conversation, coffee and a glass of something cold. Your clients should feel part of something. Of course, there's a balance to strike here too. If they haven't bought a button for months, perhaps it's time for a reminder that you're an enterprise, not just a convivial hang-out.

1. **Curb your enthusiasm**

2. **Presentation matters**

3. **The customer is sometimes wrong**

4. Hire judiciously

5. Reward loyalty

6. Lead by example

7. Don't be afraid to sell

8. Be a social linchpin

5.
Do some good

Don't forget that running a business can be your chance to give back to the community. After all, isn't your venture also about something bigger?

DO THE RIGHT THING
A guide to telling your story ethically
by Genelle Aldred

The expert: A former newsreader and journalist for the BBC, Aldred is now head of communications at The Pipeline and runs GA\C, a communications consultancy.

The lesson: Storytelling is a fundamental part of human communication and it's the best way for brands and businesses to connect meaningfully with their audience. Just make sure you're doing it right.

As businesses move towards proving their environmental, social and governance (ESG) credentials and showing they're getting it right on diversity and inclusion, we should all start to think about telling stories more ethically.

Imagine if you forgot your lunch money one day and someone lends you €10. They then go on to tell everyone about how they transformed your day (maybe even the rest of your life) because they gave you the cash to buy lunch. Next this person snaps a picture of you and the lunch and uploads their version of the story online.

How would you feel about the framing of that story? This is how organisations can appear if they don't approach stories with nuance and complexity. Business, audience

and story have never been closer; thanks to digital channels, everyone can see what has been said and how a story has been framed, while social media gives everyone recourse. Going viral because someone is unhappy with how they've been portrayed can be highly damaging to a brand. This is a real risk if businesses continue as if they are in a world of shifting power dynamics.

So how can you ensure your business tells stories ethically? Primarily it is about considering the person or community that is at the focal point. Many businesses are focused, rightly, on what they're trying to do, say or sell but we should also look through the lens of the person or community we are speaking about.

In storytelling, we can't tell it all, there's not enough space. But we can consider and think about the best way to tell a story that still promotes our product or business but doesn't make the other person a helpless victim. When the focal point of the story reads, sees or hears it, it should be an accurate representation of the situation – and it should make everyone look good.

So what can we do now? Firstly, imagine you are the focus of your brand's story. Does it feel good to hear your story this way? Secondly, never use the phrase 'voice for the voiceless.' No one is voiceless, and when we say we are their voice, we are removing their agency. We can push those voices forward and encourage our audience to listen. Finally, have diversity in your teams who tell your stories and listen to them when objections are raised at the framing of stories. If you hire to assimilate, the cycle of unethical storytelling continues. Inclusion without equity doesn't bring change.

from Stacey Boyd, founder of Olivela, the luxury shopping platform.

"The idea for my business started in the unlikeliest of places. I was on an airstrip in Dadaab, Kenya – then the world's largest refugee camp – with the world's youngest Nobel Laureate, Malala Yousafzai. We were there to meet an extraordinary group of girls who were receiving a distance education from Vodafone. In that moment, I realized that talent is equally distributed, but opportunity is not. It was a lightning bolt moment: I thought, 'What if we created a multi-brand luxury site with doing good at its very core?' Olivela was born a year later, and today it donates 20 per cent of every purchase to our non-profit partners."

GREEN MACHINE
How to create a sustainable business
by Tessa Clarke

The expert: Clarke is the co-founder and CEO of Olio, an app tackling the problem of waste in the home. Since its launch in 2016, Olio has reached four million users.

The lesson: There's never been a better – or more important – time to launch a sustainable business. The world seems to have finally woken up to the climate, biodiversity and resource depletion crises and is looking for solutions. Here are some pointers on how to make your operation more eco-conscious.

1. **Get some fire in your belly**
   To give yourself the courage and conviction, start by reading Naomi Klein's book *This Changes Everything: Capitalism vs the Climate* and Paul Gilding's *The Great Disruption*. You won't fail to be galvanised.
2. **Review your company values**
   If sustainability is going to be in your company's DNA then it needs to be baked into your values too.
3. **Check your key performance indicators** (KPI)
   What gets measured gets done, so it's critical your green credentials are reflected in your company's values and core KPIs. Ideally bonuses should be linked to these too.
4. **Review your business operations**
   This may require a re-think of your business model. For example, if you sell single-use or hard-to-repair items you will need to figure out how to migrate to a re-use, rental or repair model. This may sound daunting but the key thing is to take small steps and address easy options first.
5. **Recognise it's a journey**
   Don't let a desire for perfection paralyse you into inaction. It's best to be upfront with all stakeholders including your employees, customers, suppliers, shareholders and the media.
6. **Be original**
   When it comes to communications it's all too easy to fall into the "stock sustainability" trap, which involves a sea of clichéd imagery in various shades of green and blue. There's absolutely no need to leave your brand values at the door when conveying your eco efforts – you can do better than that.
7. **Avoid "greenwashing"**
   Finally, it can be very tempting to promote your sustainability efforts and in doing so to completely overlook the other green challenges facing your business.

While it can be easy to assume that putting the environment first will come at the expense of profitability, this couldn't be further from the truth. Rapidly shifting consumer sentiment, coupled with significant technology innovation, means that businesses that aren't sustainable will very quickly lose the licence to exist. So make sure you won't be one of them and start your sustainability journey today.

Ask the experts —— Do some good

TOP TIP
Most companies can't go from zero to fully sustainable in one go: small improvements are also key

047

MISSION POSSIBLE

Make sure there is a purpose at your company's core

by Aaisha Dadral

The expert: Dadral is the co-founder of Equiano Rum, a spirits brand named after an 18th century writer, abolitionist and entrepreneur, and founder of branding studio Crave.

The lesson: Yes, you need to think about your company's finances but customers nowadays expect more. The best businesses embed an idea of a greater good into their mission. You should too.

Full disclosure, I'm an eternal optimist even on my worst days. I'm the product of a household where the partnership of profit and purpose changed lives, every single day. My self-employed parents worked hard at improving the lives of tens of thousands of children in the UK through their foster care business. Needless to say, I'm a firm believer that business and culture are forces for good: intrinsic purpose leads businesses to success, and great businesses influence culture and change the world.

My work and life have followed that philosophy. Nearing a decade of working with some of the world's best-known companies, my studio Crave aims to craft and refine brands and implores them to "move culture" and "do better". This includes creating purposeful businesses that do more to make the world a better place, encouraging clients to build causes such as diversity, equality and sustainability into the core of their idea, and championing and nurturing creatives from under-represented backgrounds.

Before Equiano Rum had a name, it had a purpose. It is named after Olaudah Equiano, an enslaved African who bought his freedom through selling rum and who went on to inform abolishment throughout the world. This purpose perfectly aligned with the beliefs I share with my three co-founders, that freedom and equality should be enjoyed by all and business has a crucial role to play. The brand consciously places philanthropy at its core – it grants 5 per cent of profits and €2 of every bottle sold through the website to ground level freedom and equality organisations.

But why does it matter? Put simply, purpose is a reason for a business to exist beyond financial gain – it's the impact we set out to have on people's lives, the world they live in and the things they believe in.

Purpose matters to your audience

The relationship between brand and consumer is no longer one way; behaviour has changed over the last decade and it is led by younger, cause-led generations who demand more from the products they buy. Consultancy firm Accenture found that 60 per cent of young consumers believe that companies should take a stand on issues such as human rights and racism, while 40 per cent of Deloitte respondents felt that a business's goal should be to "improve society". When a brand reflects a consumer's beliefs, they express loyalty and advocacy. In fact, 79 per cent of consumers are more loyal to brands with a purpose. Further than loyalty, consumers will put their money where their conscience rests: two in three people will pay more for products from brands that are committed to making a positive social impact.

Purpose matters to your team

With cause-led generations due to make up more than half the workforce by 2030, it follows that when work reflects an employee's personal values, they're happier, more productive and more settled. And they're not afraid to make career decisions with this in mind: Wespire found that today's generation is "the first to prioritise purpose over salary", reading values and mission statements to support their decisions. Knowing what to expect from an employer builds trust and trust earns loyalty. Cone Communications found that 83 per cent of employees would be more loyal to a company that helps them contribute to social and environmental issues. Wise founders will know never to underestimate the value of a happy workforce; your team are your best advocates and an inspired one will undoubtedly inspire your consumer too.

And purpose should matter to you too

Overwhelmingly positive data and success stories shouldn't drive you to prioritise purpose. With rose-tinted glasses firmly in place, a business with purpose is the only one fit for today's market. I started my companies to fix a problem or because I believed that something could be done better. I'd hazard a guess that most founders would say the same. By many standards, that's a privilege. To have a vision, convince others to help bring it to life and then have consumers pledge their allegiance by spending their hard-earned cash with us, the least we can do is care. The less warm and fuzzy take is that purpose provides you with a guiding light. It seamlessly crafts a checklist of questions to determine the outcome of any uncertainty. It also offers much-needed clarity when marketing budgets and partner demands cloud the view.

If this all sounds great and you're jotting down your intrinsic purpose, here's my two-pence on how to create a core value for your own business:

1. **Be brave**
   Make a bold statement and set out to inspire.
2. **Be clear and mean it**
   Use simple language and keep it short. Authenticity is key – from the founder through to the organisation.
3. **Express it in a way that has longevity**
   Brand purpose needs to have staying power but don't be afraid to let it evolve.
4. **Don't reverse engineer it**
   There's a big difference between marketing messaging and intrinsic purpose. A quick Google search will betray you and the celebrity endorsement you spent cash on.
5. **Bring it to life**
   Messaging and posturing are easy but nothing has value if you don't walk-the-walk. Purpose goes beyond charitable giving. If your internal culture doesn't reflect it, you'll find yourself back at a drawing board before you know it.

How to become a business activist
by Ryan Gellert

The expert: Gellert is the CEO of sustainable clothing brand Patagonia.

The lesson: So you want to change the world but you're not quite sure how. What about profits and margins? And what if your message goes against the very essence of your industry?

Why is a clothing brand like Patagonia involved in activism?
I'm not going to preach to other brands that they have to be activists – I can only tell you why we choose to be. There are two dimensions to Patagonia. One is being a responsible business. People often refer to us as leaders in sustainability. Let's be clear, we're not a truly sustainable business, despite our best efforts over the last 48 years. The external work is being part of an activist community. We're in business to save our home planet so we will offer opinions – and scathing ones at times.

Is there a risk that you are contributing to polarisation?
I don't want to be unconstructively contributing to that. But if the response is, "Shut up, let's just all be quiet and keep businesses as usual" – that's completely unacceptable. We have fouled our planet and we have a responsibility to change that. We live in a racist country [the US] that has hundreds of years of not treating all Americans as equals and we have a responsibility to contribute to changing that. Absolutely. Unequivocally.

Patagonia tells people to buy less. Some CEOs might wonder why. Can you explain your approach?
What's the scorecard we're all planning for? Is the goal that every year you're bigger and more profitable than the year before? And anything that doesn't match that simple, narrow definition is failure? The finances are a means to an end, not the other way around.

How big a part of the core business would you like to see upcycling and recycling become?
There's this broad set of services we have under the umbrella term Worn Wear, which is about helping customers to really think about the effects of their decisions. It will include rental in the future, that's a natural extension. Hopefully we can start to create greater scale around circularity and move to a much higher level of recyclability, which is deeply embedded in our business. I would like to scale it to the point where those services are cannibalising our sales of virgin product. That's the goal – we should be creating that challenge for ourselves.

> **TOP TIP**
> Sometimes the best solution for the long term is counterintuitive in the short term – don't hold back

Ask the experts —— Do some good

6.
Digital

While we're often seen trying to reduce our screen time, an online presence is part of any business. From data and websites to social media, here's how to succeed in the digital sphere.

MAP IT OUT
Let me tell you about data
by Dr Ravi Bapna

The expert: Bapna is the associate dean for executive education at the Carlson School of Management in Minnesota.

The lesson: A lot of the early decisions around a business are made following your gut instinct but there comes a point in the evolution of a venture when it's important to assess, take stock and make calculated decisions. Forecasts, predictions and opportunities can all be found hiding in sets of data that may seem inscrutable to the untrained eye. Do not be put off. Whether you've collected the information through surveys or by tracking consumer behaviour, or if you're tackling large banks of information about the market that are freely available for all to peruse, these numbers require an in-depth look – and demand experts be the judge. Not everyone is able to convert data into a strategic asset: the successful entrepreneurs of tomorrow would do well to get themselves up to speed.

1. **Lessen the load**
   Humans have great general-purpose cognitive abilities but their capacity to make sense of multi-dimensional data pales in comparison to AI. When it comes to recognising fraud, making predictions and identifying patterns, let the maths and computational skills embedded in tools such as Python do the hard work for you.

2. **Engineer properly**
   Seventy per cent of time that's spent working on an analytics project will be taken up by cleaning, integrating, aggregating and debiasing data – make sure you budget and hire for this.

3. **Take a look outside**
   Start-ups may lack extensive operational data of their own but there are a variety of publicly available data-sources that can help: Google's data explorer, Yelp and Kaggle are three great places to start.

4. **Low-hanging fruit**
   You don't need to use AI only for spectacular, future-forward functions. Much of the value from employing these methods comes from applying AI approaches to pre-existing processes in your business – and making them better. Often you can do that by processing data that most companies already have.

5. **Get the talent**
   So you need to hire staff but what are you looking for? Find someone who has a nose for interesting business opportunities, who can do extensive data engineering, build a variety of statistical models and translate these back to you in terms of company value. Good luck finding this in one person – the thing that matters most though is being given engaging problems to work on. Making data scientists run reports or simple visualisations is a quick way to lose talent.

TOP TIP
Intuition is a great way to come up with ideas but when it comes to execution, it's important to have back-up

How can I use social media to promote my business?
by Francesca Cullen and Rosie Lees

The experts: Francesca Cullen and Rosie Lees are co-founders of Nineteen94 – a London-based boutique communications agency specialising in brand strategy, PR, digital and social media management, and event production.

The lesson: Social media is an important tool for any business – big or small. With ever-changing trends and algorithms, it can seem like a daunting proposition but there are some key pillars that any business can use to make sure that it's putting itself out there and using social media to its advantage.

What do you want?
Take time to clarify your business's goals and how you would like social media to help you achieve them. Online platforms provide a digital shop-window for your business – it allows your audience to discover who you are and what you do. Are you looking to sell your products, generate leads, build brand awareness or drive traffic to your website? Figure out what you want to achieve and spend your time efficiently across your chosen platforms.

Speak to the right people
This will impact which social media platforms you should focus your time and energy on, what kind of content you will create and what your tone of voice will be. Where does your target audience spend their time online, where will they find you and what kind of interaction do you want to have with them? Social media provides a direct link between you and your customers and this allows your business to have a personality.

Put in the effort
Once you've clarified your goals, identified your target audience and what platforms of social media they use, it's time to create your content. This should be authentic, engaging and provide value. Spend time crafting quality text that your audience actually wants to engage with. Solve a problem for them. But be mindful not to overpromote.

Be social
It's called "social media" for a reason – so make sure that you're engaging with your followers. Replying to their comments and queries, interacting with what they're posting and inspiring conversation will help you build an online community.

> **TOP TIP**
> Pre-planning and strategy are important but make sure to speak to your network the way you want to be spoken to

Why you need a standout website
by Jiahui Tan

The expert: Tan is the founder of Fable, a design practice based in Singapore that works with clients including Google, Rolex, Under Armour and more.

The lesson: A website is an indispensable tool for any business, whether you run a neighbourhood café or a boutique gallery. It may well be the first contact a customer has with your brand, so make sure it looks good – here's how.

1. **Screen**
   Most of the information we process today reaches us through screens, displayed on pixels in billboards, laptops and phones. Your customers are likely going to discover you digitally – and that's where web design comes in: it communicates visually what your product or service is all about. Find the type of aesthetic that your audience responds to and build a screen to reflect it back to them. What this looks like should be tuned to your customers' tastes – build a screen that mirrors them.

2. **Surprise**
   A great design creates a sense of discovery, providing interaction that the audience doesn't expect. In fact, interactivity is one of the tenets of a great website. With social media, we live in an age of participation where information is disseminated not just through a one-way street. And it can take many forms. Simple elements like photo galleries, social sharing buttons, animation and hover effects on links or images can make an impact. Surprise your audience with a memorable experience.

3. **Stick to it**
   Once you have narrowed down an aesthetic that works for you, stick to it. There can, of course, be variations but the visual identity of your website should be consistent. This aids brand recognition, so consumers are able to identify you by your attributes over competitors or other alternatives. You want to be understood. Stay consistent to your identity.

4. **Sensitivity**
   We live in a rapidly evolving landscape of connected devices where people get their information from a variety of places. It is crucial to ensure your web design works seamlessly through different platforms. Reading on a small device is that much harder if the font is tiny. Create a website that fits multiple formats.

5. **Sensibility**
   Fundamentally, web design needs to be intuitive and easy to navigate. Ensure you have a clear call to action. Whether it's to shop, sign up for a newsletter or watch a video campaign, make your point easily recognisable. Too many graphics or images will probably confuse your audience: if you have too much content on your pages people will most certainly lose interest. Find that balance.

CONNECT THE DOTS
How to succeed in digital
by Isabelle Dubern-Mallevays and Anna Zaoui

The experts: Dubern-Mallevays and Zaoui are co-founders of London-based The Invisible Collection, the leading digital platform for discovering bespoke furniture from the world's most renowned designers.

———————————————

The lesson: The secret to flourishing online is, in fact, all about people – from your customers and how you interact with them, to the team behind the screen.

1. **People first**
   Behind every digital business is a team of real-life humans. Without them, you cannot build your company nor foster growth. To make the right decisions you need to count on the right people.
2. **Tell your story**
   The most authentic way to create a connection between a product and consumer is to ensure they know the story of craftsmanship and design. The advantage of digital is that you can convey this through text and imagery.
3. **Stay in shape**
   Seamless retail operations are crucial, both to your customers and team. So keep your back-office digital landscape as integrated and efficient as your front-facing online exterior. This will enable your team to impeccably run all the operations and will bring your customers' experience to life. Be agile to change and open-minded to new solutions – your success depends on it.

4. **Personal touch**
   Despite being a digital business, human interaction is still important. In fact, it's your main asset. Ensure your clients can reach you, let them hear your voice and know that you care. Interaction is key. The same goes for your suppliers.

5. **Captivate your audience**
   Don't spend money artificially building your brand image. Instead, grow organically and remain authentic. Invest in creating tailored content rather than buying sponsored space. It's the best way to create an engaged online community.
6. **Learn with no limits**
   Be curious about everything in digital and continue to learn about the latest innovations.

FIND THE ANSWER
A guide to launching an online business
by Amelia Gain

The expert: As a former hotelier, Amelia Gain found a solution for hotel administration. This inspired her to start her New Zealand-based brand Preno, an online tool to make hoteliers' lives easier.

———————————————

The lesson: While building a bricks-and-mortar business has its challenges, creating an online one can seem far more daunting to those with little or no knowledge. It doesn't have to be as scary as you think.

When I was 23, my sister and I decided to take over The Spire, a luxury boutique hotel in the bustling tourist hotspot of Queenstown, New Zealand. Biting that bullet and taking that leap, it seems almost foolhardy when looking back. But we loved every minute of it.

While we hustled and worked to provide unparalleled experiences for our guests, I realised just how frustrating it was behind the scenes. The back-end of the website and the front of house were disparate parts, often meaning double-handling of data and increasing the odds for human error. Countless headaches and late nights filled with manual data entry proved to me there was a crucial need for a simpler solution.

And that's the key to our success. A solution, based upon years of our own blood, sweat, and tears, that meets our customers where their own needs lie. Preno software works to cut down the admin for hoteliers, saving them 10 hours a week on average, giving them valuable time back in their days to focus on customer experience. It now reaches more than 7,000 hoteliers in 25 countries and counting. It also helps save them from the outdated back-end they've dealt with for years.

Preno's key values have helped to drive this global success. A commitment to continual learning and innovation helps our product remain fit for purpose. This is reliant on clear and empathetic communication with our customers, which is mainly hinged on the brilliant staff we employ. I've always said that surrounding yourself with the top talent will net you the best results – and for us it's true.

So how should you go about developing your own online business? When developing a software product that is easy to use, you have to know your customers' problems inside and out. These insights should be blended with technical innovation to create a prototype. You must then iterate on it and release it to all customers. We talked to our market a lot in the process to make sure it was creating value for our customers.

In the early developmental stages of Preno, we spent time validating our purpose and getting customers onboard before we launched, in order to save ourselves time and money at a later stage.

I was fortunate in that my best friend and co-founder is a talented developer too – it was a huge asset for Preno. For anyone looking to build their own tech platform, my advice would be to bring in a technical partner. I know many successful companies that have used agencies or outsourced overseas but building a product is an iterative process. Development never ends, especially in SAAS (software as a service). It's important you learn along the way so that you can adapt quickly. Those learnings are then owned by you too, increasing your own technical knowledge and ability. So, my key advice to those looking to dive into the depths of a technology start-up is threefold:

1. **Be clear on the problem you're trying to solve**
   "Running a hotel is hard and a lot of our time is taken up with repetitive admin." This is the challenge that we built Preno's foundation around. We've created a powerful and effortless hotel management platform that acts as the autopilot for these properties. This base service has kickstarted our innovation in other products, such as an automation that will improve the guest experience, enabling hoteliers to grow their businesses.

2. **Validate this issue with your target customers**
   It's easy to waste time by trying to solve a problem that impacts everyone. Be clear on who it is you're helping and who has the most trouble with the problem you've already identified. This ensures you build the right product for a group of passionate early adopters.

3. **Have a crystal clear vision and laser focus on the solution you're developing**
   Developing an online business can be difficult because it's a never-ending process – you can get lost down the rabbithole with all the distractions. Maintaining focus will give you the most value. I'd also say to go with your gut – there's much to be said about instinct and usually your first idea will be right.

A WORD OF ADVICE
from Luis Von Ahn, CEO of language-learning app Duolingo

"In the first few years, we started getting more and more investment. Getting investment seems like free money at first but then you realise you're paying an exchange where you fraction ownership of your company. We decided it was time for Duolingo to start paying for itself – the only problem was that our mission is to provide language education for free. So we put an ad at the end of every lesson. Soon people started asking if they could pay to remove the ads; we added a subscription business. Now only 2 per cent of our users pay for the app but we have so many that we get more money than companies where 100 per cent of the users pay."

7.
Learn and improve

Even the most time-tested enterprise can benefit from taking a step back and reconsidering the way it operates. Here are the tips and tweaks that might just help turn a good business into a great one.

GROW YOUR OWN
How data can help you scale up your company
by Jasmin Yaya

The expert: Yaya is a Stockholm-based product manager, educator and growth coach at Scilla Studio.

The lesson: The business world is constantly evolving. That's true of every sector but for digital entreprises, the need to adapt is a perennial, existential issue. Here's how to make sure that change leads in an upwards trajectory – and is always accompanied by growth.

Every entrepreneur needs to know about their products, their customers, and the world around them to make better and faster business decisions. Still, those decisions can't be made on instinct or data alone. Relying on intuition can be misleading because we are all subject to several human biases: we often believe in an idea just because it is ours. But making conclusions solely based on data also has its problems – data is by definition historical. That's why we need to equip ourselves with an efficient tool to make conclusions – that tool is experimentation. However, it's likely that only one in three new ideas will give a desired outcome so learn to test your hypotheses to understand what works and what doesn't. And remember,

it's impossible to do it on your own: the secret is to work with your team. Ultimately, a successful entrepreneur is someone who's willing to learn and focus on critical areas for growth. These outcomes can ensure a strong future for your digital company.

Retention
The key to sustainable growth is retaining customers – not just acquiring new ones. In the case of an app, for example, it's normal to lose 80 per cent of new users within seven days. The one-week window is fundamental to obtain better results and grow faster than the competition. Ask yourself how customers can find out the value of your product sooner – and at which point they lose interest.

Monetisation
Understand when the best time to generate revenue is – and how to do it. Is it best to offer a subscription or to opt for a one-time payment?

Acquisition
Distribution has become more competitive, expensive and challenging. Social media ad costs are rising, click-through rates are down and marketers cannot target customers as before. Always keep your audience in mind as they will be instrumental to your growth: is there a way to make sure that current users can help attract new customers by simply using your product? If not, design it so they will.

> **TOP TIP**
> Growth can be organic but it doesn't just happen – help it along by studying what you've already got

How to ensure the wellbeing of your teams
by Markus Albers

The expert: Markus Albers is co-founder and managing partner at Berlin-based consultancy Rethink, where he manages the welfare of his 50 employees.

The lesson: Ensuring your team are on top form mentally is something that managers need to take into consideration. But what's the best way to go about it?

In the old days, the idea of caring for the wellbeing of one's employees amounted to offering challenging projects alongside smart colleagues, providing a tasteful office environment and having a bottle of white wine in the fridge for the occasional aperitivo.

Unfortunately the trend towards remote working means that things have gotten a little more complicated. Now managers need to consider how to care for the psychological stability of team members that may be holed away in their home office in another city – or another country for that matter.

In fact, keeping up morale and providing what HR-types call "culture" has gotten exponentially harder. The projects may still be challenging but your fancy office doesn't show on Zoom. And virtual Friday afternoon drinks with everyone alone in front of their screens just feels a little sad.

It's harder to unite your troops behind company goals when most of them work with a laptop on their terrace. Employees that need no longer commute to your HQ may consider other places to work – even far away from where they live.

A client of our agency, who works as head of people and organisational development at a big financial services firm, told me that her company's answer was an online program around mindfulness. Employees trained with a coach or meditated using audio files.

Not all employees will appreciate such wandering by their superiors in what they might consider private territory. In any case, too much digital prodding can turn into the opposite of the desired effect. According to studies, around 84 per cent of employees are permanently on standby. Another 80 per cent say they suffer from stress – more than ever before. Health insurers warn that there is a causal link between the new "always-on" culture of working and the increasing number of stress-related illnesses.

Driven by technology, the omnipresence of work will increase. Soon, smart glasses and virtual assistants may put a permanent digital layer between us and reality. Politics seems to wake up to that threat: French workers have had the right to disconnect since 2016. Similar legislation is being discussed in the EU Parliament.

If you would rather not see politics meddling in your internal processes, you should adopt some sensible policies before regulation happens. Your teams should make it transparent when and on which channels they can be reached and with what response time. Managers must learn to communicate much more asynchronously – less interrupting employees with phone calls and meetings. And everyone must agree on longer periods of uninterrupted concentration.

In the end, though, the best way to ensure a healthy work culture is probably the old one: provide employees with a nice office to retreat to for at least part of the week. Allow for some socialising. And crack open that bottle of white from time to time.

TOP TIP
It's the key rule of storytelling: without conflict, a story doesn't develop – and your business won't either

A WORD OF ADVICE
from Debbie Wosskow, co-founder of members club Allbright

"As founders, our entrepreneurial mindset means that we're constantly looking for new opportunities and problems to solve. It is about harnessing the skills typically associated with business owners: a strong sense of vision, dogged hard graft, and our creative flair and ability to do and see things differently. Day by day, week by week. Some of the best ideas emerge from challenging situations."

Ask the experts ——— Learn and improve

GOING GLOBAL

Expanding into international markets

by Maria Hatzistefanis

The expert: Hatzistefanis is founder and CEO of Rodial, a skincare brand she launched in 1999 with a small investment. She has since managed the company's expansion into 35 countries.

The lesson: You've made it big in your local community. Where next? Branching into new markets is a great way to continue growing and getting your name out there. So what are you waiting for?

Why should you consider expanding globally?
For two reasons. First there are only so many sales that you can generate in one country and every new area that you expand into generates incremental revenue and helps the business grow. Secondly, the impact of a brand's online presence is global and so too is their community. At Rodial, we reach customers in over 60 countries. Unless we capitalise on this international brand awareness by having our products available internationally this is a missed opportunity.

How do you know if your brand is ready?
Export can be quite complicated – it can involve setting international prices, negotiating contracts with distributors and, in certain cases, having to register products in a new market. You do need to have a solid team and someone strong on operations and finance who can help navigate this tricky process. I started expanding Rodial in year three when I had both an operations and finance director to support me in the venture.

What are the benefits and drawbacks?
The pros are additional revenue and increased brand awareness. The image of the company needs to be controlled and it should be represented in a similar way to the home market. From visuals to the tone of voice – and if there is a physical store presence – everything needs to remain in line with the brand identity. Rodial has a team that communicates all our assets, display specs and tone of voice ensuring consistency across the board.

How does running a global brand differ?
It is important to understand the customer in each country and the appetite for your firm. You should also be aware of the distribution network and how your company can fit in. If we're selling a luxury product and there is no luxury distribution channel in a certain country then we won't expand there. There are other countries where the import duties are extremely high. We would need to increase our prices dramatically to enter the market but then we wouldn't be competitive.

How do you scale up your team to fit your business's new reach?
At Rodial I hired a sales manager very early on who was responsible for all sales including everything international. We then added more people to the team when the extra support was needed. My way of doing business is more organic and I hire when the needs arise.

What advice would you give to someone looking to expand?
Start with a country that you know well. Learn all you need to – from both successes and challenges – and then move on to the next.

"What does it mean to be 'authentic' when it comes to supporting a cause? To start, it's useful to consider your motivations. Education is also key: improving our knowledge of the challenges a community faces helps us determine where best to direct our efforts. There are two main methods: material action (through fundraising) and a proactive approach (to shifting diversity). Is your business physically improving life for the people you wish to support? This could include donating a portion of profits to a charity or driving attention to an issue that's not widely understood. And is your brand being reactive? Are you actively showing commitment year-round?"

Lessons for a four-day week
by Elvire Jaspers

The expert: Jaspers is the co-founder of WeAreBrain, a digital and technology agency based in Amsterdam. After successfully running and selling her first start-up in 2017, she has been involved in numerous digital ventures.

The lesson: Flexible working can be a boon to wellbeing and productivity but it should be flexible in its implementation too.

In 2014 I launched WeAreBrain with my co-founders Mario Grunitz and Jack Myasushkin. We decided early on that we would be open to all types of working arrangements. It made sense for us as we were all based in different countries. The company has grown dramatically since but everyone still has a flexible schedule. Of course our policy also needs to match the needs of our clients and company. And it's not as straightforward as simply announcing it as a policy and expecting it all to fall into place. The way that our company works has been great for us and our employees – and has proved to be successful. But it takes a lot of thought and planning, and a willingness to make it work.

Get organised
Flexible-working arrangements require a lot of planning. If your company has people who are not working on certain days, you have to organise that within a team so that ongoing projects are always covered. But it's about creating schedules for people too. You need to take a deeper interest as a manager in what your employees need as individuals – whether that's more structure or freedom. You then have to connect your company goals with a purpose, weaving company values into daily work tasks. Your employees will be happier and more productive for it.

Improve communication
We have found that as long as you explain your policy to clients and ensure they know that they will always be covered, most of them are happy. But it's all about transparency. It's also important to give people the right tools to actually work together and to share information so that nobody is left out of the communication process. This is particularly important. It is then crucial for managers to ask their team for regular feedback. You might not get it right the first time – so you should be prepared to make multiple attempts before you do.

Change the way that you measure success
There are so many people out there who are in an office, sitting at a desk for eight hours, from nine-to-five. And what's their overall output? It's still questionable. You have to shift away from the belief that long hours spent in the office are a measure of a job well done; for us it's about a project being delivered successfully and efficiently. What we have seen is that if you give employees confidence and trust them to make it happen then the number of hours that they work becomes irrelevant. For us, success is measured by the velocity of the team and by the output we see.

Be realistic
Allowing employees to have flexible working arrangements will vary depending on the company, the industry and your firm's goals. We are very open to flexible schedules because we are a technology agency. If you're, for example, a car-making factory, then your flexible arrangements will look very different. But that doesn't mean it's not possible; companies can experiment with shift work or shortened days. You just have to figure out how it can work for you.

SILVER LINING
What I learnt when my business failed
by Ruth Barry

The expert: Barry was a project manager before she launched Black Isle Bakery in Berlin in 2012. She closed the shop in 2021 and is now onto her next venture.

The lesson: Failure is an experience that no entrepreneur wants to encounter, yet one that pretty much every one will in some way or the other. But it's what you do next that matters.

In 2021, I closed my bakery. I remember how I felt starting out in 2012, I'd found purpose after years of feeling inadequate and it awoke an unyielding determination in me.

I was ready for hard work but I felt trapped in what I'd created, turned loose from all that I loved about baking. Something needed to change. I asked myself what I was prepared to accept in order to be free of it all. I was ready to accept insolvency. I hadn't paid myself for almost a year, I had little left to lose. I realised that the spirit of the bakery lay in me. Even if my shop closed, I would find another way to continue sharing what I do. There was a time when I thought the world would stop turning if I lost my business. I never imagined the sense of relief that would come in the end. I now know what matters to me and I'm using that to map out new ideas. I believe that knowledge is for sharing, so I've started writing a recipe book and will soon set up a new digital channel where I'll publish tutorials, recipes and other meanderings. I'm closing the door on this chapter, but I'll let my curiosity inspire me and my experience guide me as I write the first lines of a new beginning.

> **TOP TIP**
> Expecting an entrepreneurial journey to be free of failure is unrealistic. The key is how you react

YOU'RE HIRED
Attracting talent
by Cynthia Hansen

The expert: Hansen heads the Adecco Group Foundation, the social impact arm of the Adecco Group, the world's leading HR-solutions firm.

The lesson: Work means many things to many people but it's the manner of your approach to the daily grind – your ambitions, your colleagues and your routine – that will define your career.

Talented, talentless, a rising talent. As the lines between industries and sectors blur, talent becomes fluid. A top coder will be pursued by both banks and technology firms. An engineer might be snapped up by a logistics company. Where do you find them? And from whom do you lure them away?

As businesses go global they struggle to navigate the complexities of finding and attracting talent. Moving off home turf into new markets means facing unfamiliar market conditions, new labour and tax regulations, different cultural norms and language barriers. Do you retreat to what you know by bringing your own staff and methods (and possibly bias)? Or leave yourself at the mercy of the market? The answer is neither and both. Tomorrow's competitive company won't be staffed with drag-and-drop talent. Instead it requires a dynamic mix that allows flexibility and quick scaling, builds bench depth, provides career paths and enriches communities. This is the Adecco Group's Triple B talent framework: Bring, Buy and Build. Think of it as a set of questions that help you determine the right mix. First, be clear what you are trying to achieve. Then define the kind of operations required and the timeframe. To ensure a strategic choice, try this simple approach.

1. **Bring**
   If the skills are too specialised to exist in the local market and there isn't a critical mass of possible trainees, consider bringing your own staff. Do you have a short timeline? Are labour costs prohibitive? Is there a lack of training capacity?

2. **Buy**
   The skills you need might already exist – but if they do you could face fierce competition. Why would candidates choose you over a competitor? Buy might offer more stability but comes with broader obligations.

3. **Build**
   If local candidates don't have what you need but are trainable, you might consider Build. How quickly can they be skilled up? Do they have the propensity to learn the skills you need? Will they be valuable to you in the future? Build is a long-term investment and might require interim solutions. It adds the most enrichment to the labour pool.

How to be a good boss
by Kim Scott

The expert: Scott is co-founder of Candor Inc and the author of best-selling book *Radical Candor*.

The lesson: Being able to rely on a good team is half the battle when it comes to running a company. All you have to do first is nail the "boss" business first.

Early in my career I was an entrepreneur. I founded a couple of sales start-ups before joining Google where I realised that what got me up in the morning was building a great team. Steve Jobs had decided that Apple was going to throw out its management training and start over so I developed a course called Managing at Apple for it. I realised that managing there was similar to managing anywhere. So I started writing my book, *Radical Candor*, because the advice I was giving to technology CEOs was the same that I gave to young people just starting out.

As a manager you need to care personally about your employees while also challenging them. That's 'radical candour'. If you challenge someone but don't show that you care about them, that's 'obnoxious aggression'. Having a senior leader who behaves this way creates a culture of fear.

But it's also one of the mistakes we most fear making. Often when we realise we've been a jerk, we move in the wrong direction. We say we "didn't really mean it" or "it's no big deal" when, in fact, we did mean it and it is a big deal – and we end up in the worst place of all. The majority of mistakes are made when somebody is so worried about not hurting someone's feelings that they don't tell them something they would be better off knowing. This happens all the time at work: mistakes that don't get corrected get repeated.

There is a path that companies often go down. A successful small company is often very candid. People know each other well and part of the reason that they're successful is that they deal with things as they arise. But as they have success, they grow and want to maintain that nice culture – that sense of almost being a family – but now they don't know people as well so they tend to pull their punches. They no longer point out problems like they did before so you get this culture of what I call "ruinous empathy", which can lead to failure.

It's easy for me to say, "Be radically candid", but how do you do it? Here is how.

1. **Solicit feedback**
   This is true no matter where you are in the hierarchy but it's especially important if you're the boss. You need to understand what is going on from other perspectives.
2. **Focus on the good stuff**
   If you're a leader, especially an entrepreneur, your job is to show your team what's possible. Praise is a much better tool for doing this than criticism. Remember that praise has to be sincere and specific. One of the mistakes people make is thinking that praise is only used to show that you care about someone when it should also challenge other people directly: it shows the whole team what success looks like.
3. **Now you're in a better place to offer criticism**
   Make sure that while you praise in public, you criticise in private. The best criticism I've ever received has come in impromptu two-minute conversations. It can be a gift in one of two ways: either because you're giving the person an opportunity to fix the problem or because you're wrong and only by telling that person what you think do you give them the opportunity to correct your thinking. But remember to state that you're giving criticism to help them improve. Make sure you do it right away. The longer you wait, the harder it is to remember the context.
4. **Focus on things people can change**
   Describe the situation, the behaviour and the impact that the behaviour had. Then you're explaining to the person how to change the way they do things, not their personality.

In early 2000s, a lawyer friend said that in Silicon Valley, management is neither taught nor rewarded. The good news is that that has started to change. There is an increasing understanding that getting management right is the only way you can build the product or service you're passionate about. For entrepreneurs it's really easy to get caught up in the stress – there's no more stressful job out there – but if you can get the management side right then the stress goes down and the product gets better. And most importantly, the relationships will be fun.

Ask the experts ——— Learn and improve

How to make an inherited business your own

by Sofia and Lucila Pescarmona

The experts: Sofia is the president and CEO of Bodega Lagarde, a business that she inherited. She is also on the board of directors of Wines of Argentina. Lucila lives in San Francisco where she oversees new business development and the brand's exports.

The lesson: While it may not involve starting a firm from scratch, there's plenty to be said for the inherited business. Playing the generation game has its own challenges, from opinionated family members to old-fashioned methods of working.

Our generation's story of continuing the family business started in 2001 after Argentina's deepest economic, social and political crisis. Sofia quit her job in a leading telecommunications company for where she had worked for eight years. She asked for permission to manage the family winery. Bodega Lagarde had started small mostly as a passion project for our parents. They had invested money from other businesses in planting a vineyard and were committed to turning the century-old facility into an exceptional producer of terroir-driven wines – similar to the ones they had admired in France, Italy and other countries.

Sofia went all in at 28-years-old with the illusion of making fast and furious changes to a historical company. Not only did she encounter many challenges, like culture clashes between her corporate-background mentality and rural dormancy but also her lack of understanding of the long-term process involved in making great wine. Our father Enrique once told her, you cannot measure

yourself in the wine business in two or three years, rather 10 to 15. Only then you will know if you are on the right track.

At first, Sofia didn't believe our father when it came to making these changes in wine styles, vineyard management, viticulture and importers. It took her five years to understand the industry, its players, nuances and then another five to understand her palate and fall in love with the uncertainty of being in an agricultural business. Eventually, she learned from her own mistakes.

Twelve years into Sofia's management of the company, I joined the team to help Sofia run the winery. I brought my own ambitions of what to pursue. But together we settled into a mission of making exceptional terroir wines from Argentina – and we also wanted to support our community and environment.

Sofia became interested in local flora and fauna and developed her passion for conservation and eventually worked to bring it into winemaking and sustainable agriculture. Having grown up in Mendoza and being extremely proud of my heritage, I knew that Bodega Lagarde and the community had to be well-integrated. We wanted to share the Mendoza lifestyle with the world but also be proud ambassadors for our wines, our land and our people.

During all the years since taking over the family business, we've learned that the winery and its wines had to reflect our own tastes and what was happening in our own personal lives at the time. But it also meant finding a fine balance between our own goals and the respect for those who came before us. We wanted the winery to be a continuation of its history but also of the future. We will be able to measure our success if the next generation will be able to inherit a winery that is successful in numbers but also in its legacy.

PART 2.

FIND YOUR PATCH

So you've had some thoughts about turning your hobby into a vocation but isn't it time you thought about which city (or town or fishing village) will serve you best in the long run? Video-calling and emails will only help convey your message so far. It's time to consider somewhere to set up shop with connections to investors, customers or even competitors.

That said, you've taken the risk of doing things on your own terms – and you should get something out of the bargain for yourself. Perhaps you'll look for a walkable city small enough for you to amble home for lunch with the family. Or rather a town within striking distance of the slopes for a weekend skiing trip. Whatever you decide, it should work for you and the business.

Remember to think about how to scale up the operation if things go well and how to achieve a balance. Your new base should be in an area you love but it should also be able to support you (personally and professionally). Here we set forth to discover the essence of a few key cities and lesser-known locales for you to try out before you put in an offer.

Find your patch

Seeking a spot to start your new venture?
We've scoured the globe in search of the places
with big business potential and a great quality
of life – whether it's a thriving metropolis,
compact city or rural outpost you're after.

NETHERLANDS

Amsterdam

The bike-loving city that offers plenty of start-up success

The Dutch capital's pretty canals and rich history have always been a big draw for tourists. But its relaxed feel and enviable quality of life mean a growing number of entrepreneurs are putting down roots too. The city is now Europe's fourth-biggest start-up hub, as well as being home to tech brands such as WeTransfer and streaming giant Netflix's European headquarters.

Amsterdam allows great work-life balance; it's green, most residents speak English and many cultural events are accessible to an international audience. The city is compact enough to get around by bike and excellent public transport makes getting out of town easy too. The beach is just 20 minutes away and high-speed connections take you to Brussels, Paris and London.

Business-wise, it makes sense too. Registering a company is easy, the government supports start-up visas and skilled expats qualify for a discount on income tax. The city has invested in being an attractive place to start or grow your business; there are plenty of co-working spaces as well as academies, accelerators and incubators to help new businesses thrive. And it has paid off: Dutch tech companies punch above their weight when it comes to raising funding.

Key facts:
Population: 873,290
Key trades: Electronics, automobile industry, shipping, agriculture, hospitality, tech, finance, media
Time it takes to register a new business: 10 to 14 days
Closest airport: Amsterdam Schiphol Airport has non-stop passenger flights to 267 destinations in 84 countries, plus 3 domestic routes
Average wage: €31/hour
Cost of office space: €221/sq m
Average property price: €520,000
Cost of a beer: €5
Hours of sunlight per year: 1,662

Find your patch —— Where to set up

USA
Los Angeles
The glitzy metropolis with a creative streak and a sunny disposition

Summing up Los Angeles in a few words can be tricky due to the multiple personalities it displays but this constantly sunny, perennially laidback city enjoys an enviable location – and it's easy to see why it lures creative talent from across the US and beyond. Boasting a vibrant fashion and design industry, a thriving culinary and hospitality scene and home to a growing number of tech firms, it has established itself as something of a magnet for entrepreneurs. Between its bountiful customer base (more than 45 million people visit annually, in addition to its 10 million permanent residents) and plethora of government incentives, new business owners will find plenty of support here.

It also fosters and encourages innovation. With its most successful enterprises linked to the arts, Los Angeles is the perfect place to test a non-traditional idea that perhaps wouldn't work elsewhere. What's more, the city is home to a thriving community of creatives offering endless networking opportunities. Then of course, there's the beach – or perhaps deserts, mountains, waterfalls or lakes are more your bag: the city has it all (and more) within striking distance.

Key facts:

Population: 10 million

Key trades: Entertainment, film, tech, hospitality, business and professional management services, health services and research, trade and tourism

Time it takes to register a new business: 4 weeks

Closest airport: Los Angeles International Airport has non-stop passenger flights to 192 international destinations in 39 countries, plus 118 domestic routes

Average wage: €25.80/hour

Cost of office space: €408/sq m

Average property price: €633,000

Cost of a beer: €5.90

Hours of sunlight per year: 3,254

London
The financial and cultural powerhouse that's a world in microcosm

"When a man is tired of London, he is tired of life," said playwright and author Samuel Johnson in 1777. It's a maxim that still rings true today. London is a vast, unknowable city brimming with opportunity. Granted, it may not be cheap but when it comes to access to capital, investment and global talent London is the place to be. Despite the wobbles of Brexit, the UK capital remains a financial juggernaut and home to the likes of Citibank, Barclays and HSBC – not to mention the London Stock Exchange, which is the world's most international exchange. London start-ups have gained €29bn in investment since 2016 and the average seed round (a financing round that raises initial capital to start a business) stands at €550,000 compared with the global average of €420,000.

However, London's biggest draw is arguably its cultural scene. It attracts the biggest international talent to its world-leading museums, galleries, music venues and performance spaces – making it near impossible to be bored. And you'll be in good company, too. From internationally renowned architects and designers to publishers and poets, some of the biggest names in every industry have made the city their home so get ready for some serious networking.

Key facts:

Population: 9.4 million

Key trades: Professional, scientific and technical services, finance and insurance, culture, media, information and communication

Time it takes to register a new business: 24 hours

Closest airport: London has five main airports – the largest, London Heathrow has non-stop passenger flights to 240 international destinations in 90 countries, plus 9 domestic routes

Average wage: €21/hour

Cost of office space: €591/sq m

Average property price: €600,000

Cost of a beer: €6.20

Hours of sunlight per year: 1,481

Find your patch —— Where to set up

AUSTRALIA

Adelaide

The underdog that's powering ahead with a wealth of investment

For years the South Australian capital had been almost forgotten by the rest of the country. In the meantime, Adelaide was quietly building its own fortune. It has boomed thanks to local companies that pick up defence contracts, the relocation of the nation's space agency from Canberra, the country's most prolific cluster of wine regions and a packed cultural calendar. There's also a host of excellent nightspots to boot.

Adelaide initially grew out of British wealth in the late 19th and early 20th centuries and then saw major investment again during the 1970s thanks to the car-manufacturing industry. This series of economic highs can be seen in the skyline of stately colonial-era builds and bulky brutalist blocks. And the current boom is marked by cranes on the horizon, which are building €2.2bn worth of city infrastructure and commercial developments. This renewal has been aided by industry-led non-profit initiatives such as Renew Adelaide, through which a network of property owners provides subsidies to fill empty lots with young entrepreneurs who want to test their food or retail concepts. It's a smart move for a state that has in the past lost its young talent.

Key facts:

Population: 26,177

Key trades: Public administration, professional scientific and technical services

Time it takes to register a new business: 2 to 5 days

Closest airport: Adelaide Airport has non-stop passenger flights to 29 destinations in 6 countries, plus 23 domestic routes

Average wage: €30/hour

Cost of office space: €334/sq m

Average property price: €443,000

Cost of a beer: €5

Hours of sunlight per year: 2,516

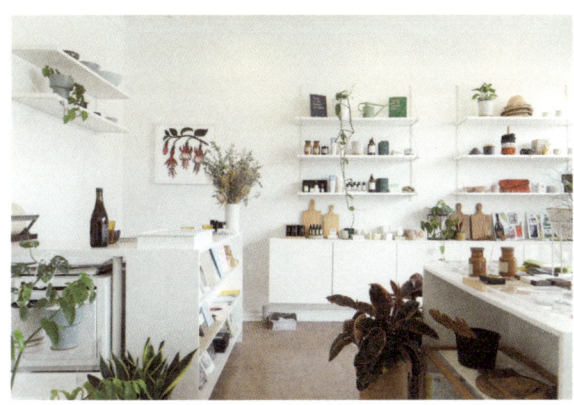

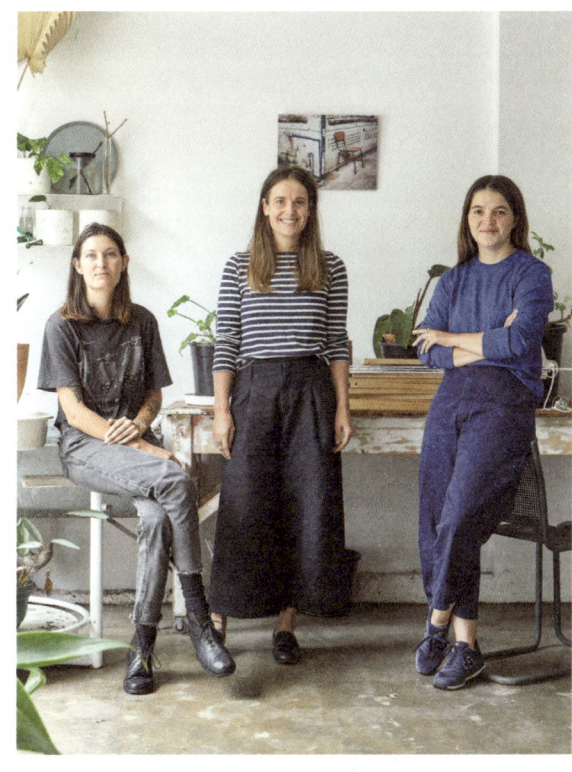

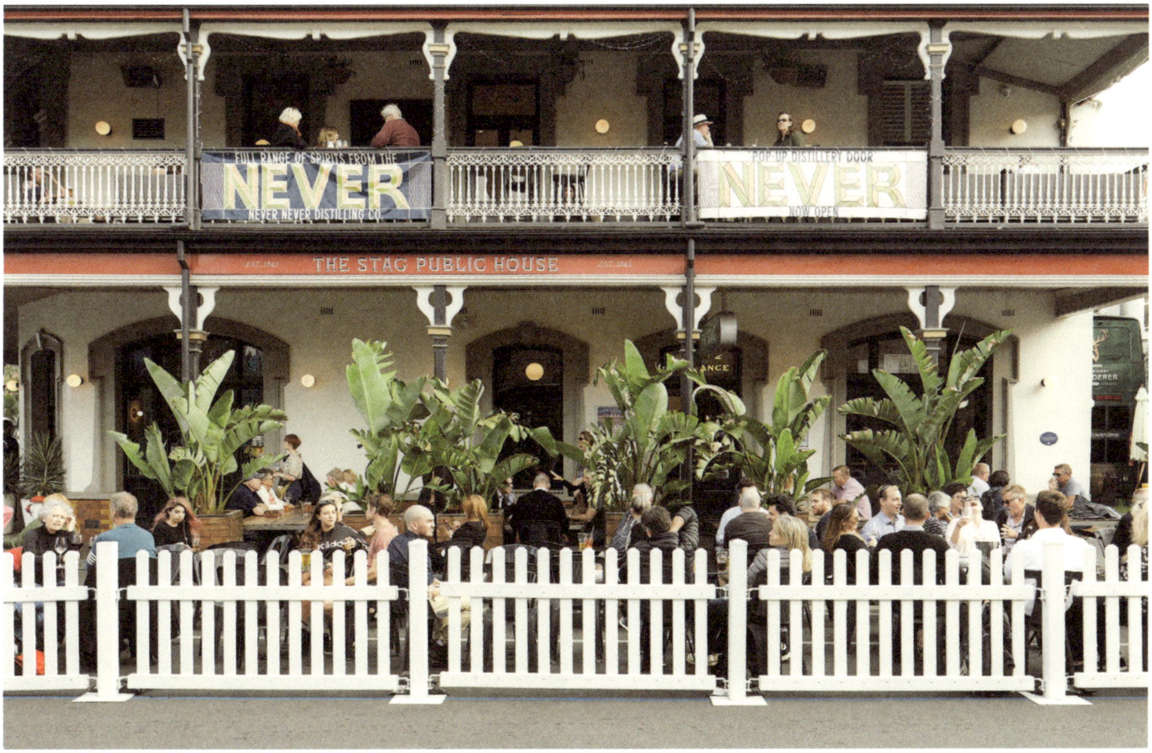
FULL RANGE OF SPIRITS FROM THE
NEVER
NEVER NEVER DISTILLING CO.
POP-UP DISTILLERY DOOR
NEVER
NOW OPEN
THE STAG PUBLIC HOUSE

JAPAN
Hiroshima
The characterful Japanese city brimming with potential

Perched on a delta that empties into the Seto Inland Sea, this spacious, verdant city in the west of Japan has a population just shy of 1.2 million. Its lack of density makes it manageable and everything – from the traffic to the old-fashioned trams – seems to move at a gentler pace. Just over an hour's flight from Tokyo (and also connected by shinkansen), Hiroshima has easy access to the capital. The city's notorious history – it is one of two cities on which the US dropped an atomic bomb – also forms the basis for a thriving tourism industry that pulls in 13 million visitors a year.

Hiroshima would make a great place to start a hospitality business and with all the forests nearby it's good for furniture-making and architecture too. The retail scene is creative, while subsidies are on offer for new businesses. The city sees no need for breakneck development and for some it's the proximity to nature that makes it such an attractive place to live and work. Coastal diving opportunities, pristine fishing spots and forest hiking trails are all within an hour's drive. Farms and orchards blanket the northern mountains and neighbouring islands, while the coastline is Japan's top oyster-producing region.

Key facts:

Population: 1.2 million	
Key trades: Wholesale/retail, manufacturing, real estate	
Time it takes to register a new business: 1 week	
Closest airport: Hiroshima Airport has non-stop passenger flights to 7 international destinations, plus 5 domestic routes	
Average wage: €18.50/hour	
Cost of office space: €334/sq m	
Cost of a beer: €3.70	
Hours of sunlight per year: 2,042	

Find your patch — Where to set up

FINLAND
Helsinki
The Nordic start-up hub where fresh thinking can flourish

The Finnish capital offers a vibrant scene for entrepreneurs and – due to events such as Slush, Europe's biggest start-up gathering – attracts capital far beyond its size. In recent years the city has given rise to several international growth companies in sectors ranging from technology to biomaterials, as well as those drawing on Finland's rich design heritage. The openness for innovation and ideas is rooted in Finland's recent history. The country transformed itself from an agriculture and forestry-based economy into an IT powerhouse that gave birth to the likes of Nokia. Today, it's a truly international city with a high level of English-speaking residents and a handy geographical position allowing for excellent flight connections to Europe, the US and Asia.

Mayor Jan Vapaavuori also believes that a high quality of life is good for business. "Younger generations don't think, 'Which company do I want to work for?'" he says, "More, 'Which city do I want to live in?'" Not only is Helsinki a highly functional city with efficient public transport and easy access to forests and coastline, but the Finnish government supplies ample support to young companies in the form of grants and impressive tax-based incentives to help innovators really pick up speed.

Key facts:

Population: 650,000

Key trades: Financial, administrative and business services

Time it takes to register a new business: roughly 2 weeks

Closest airport: Helsinki Airport has non-stop flights to 117 destinations in 44 countries, plus 16 domestic routes

Average wage: €29/hour

Cost of office space: €33.50/sq m

Cost of a beer: €6.50

Hours of sunlight per year: 1,802

Find your patch —— Where to set up

MOROCCO

Tangier

The well-connected coastal city where business is booming

Europe's gateway to Africa, Tangier bridges the two continents seamlessly: mosques cosy up to catholic cathedrals and cafés spill out onto the pavement next to traditional markets. Socialites and creative folk have long been drawn to the city for its freewheeling reputation, pleasant climate and colourful cultural scene. But where hippies used to come in search of easy living, now entrepreneurs are seeking to invest.

The past few decades have seen Moroccan King Mohammed VI unwavering in his dedication to updating Tangier into a modern beach town and thriving international business centre. He has instigated large-scale infrastructure projects including Tangier Med Harbour, a new port just outside the city providing connections to 186 ports in 77 countries. This has served to solidify Tangier's position as an attractive location for companies wanting to export into markets across Africa and Europe.

Another boost came in 2018 with the completion of Africa's first high-speed rail link between Tangier and Casablanca. These projects have helped it grow from being Morocco's fifth-largest city (in terms of GDP) in 2005 to the second largest today. While Casablanca might still be in the lead as the country's main business hub, Tangier certainly comes first in terms of charm and potential.

Key facts:

Population: 995,000	
Key trades: Agriculture, tourism	
Time it takes to register a new business: 7 to 10 days	
Closest airport: Tangier Ibn Battouta Airport has non-stop passenger flights to 30 destinations in 8 countries, plus 4 domestic routes	
Average wage: €4.50/hour	
Cost of a beer: €2.50	
Hours of sunlight per year: 2,974	

SWITZERLAND
Basel
The business-savvy border-city where the living is easy

Basel is equal parts classic Swiss charm – complete with cobbled streets and wooden-shuttered buildings – and multinational industry concerned with Pritzker prize-winning architects designing their corporate campuses. Novartis, Roche and other business giants nestle into the corner of the Rhine where Germany, France and Switzerland meet. Basel is both an industrial powerhouse and a waterside paradise, complete with its own "Rhyviera". The Rhine is the same, wide and wild, but it's also controlled and split into channels for leisure, pleasure and transport.

Basel is known in the cultural and luxury worlds for Art Basel and Baselworld but the city is vibrant year-round. It has a European panache that mixes all its neighbouring influences, best reflected in the city's museums and architecture; a bike trip around the centre will reveal many feats by the native powerhouse Herzog & de Meuron. Meanwhile, a prominent pharmaceutical and med-tech sector has made the city a life-sciences centre, and the canton is the most business-friendly in already business-friendly Switzerland. Moreover, its attempts to be the first city in the country to introduce paternity leave is proof of its progressive spirit.

Key facts:

Population: 195,844

Key trades: Life sciences, arts and culture

Closest airport: EuroAirport Basel Mulhouse Freiburg has non-stop passenger flights to 13 destinations in 7 countries

Average wage: €23/hour

Cost of office space: €218/sq m

Average property price: €980,200

Cost of a beer: €7

Hours of sunlight per year: 1,640

VIETNAM
Ho Chi Minh City
The buzzing metropolis where young entrepreneurs can get a leg up

Ho Chi Minh City is undergoing a cultural renaissance led by a young, tech-savvy and optimistic population. With Vietnam's average age sitting at a mere 30 and the government successfully opening up the country to investment, creative entrepreneurs are finding a foothold here. A dynamic and cosmopolitan place, Ho Chi Minh City is fast-paced, bursting with noisy, vibrant street life and a palpable entrepreneurial spirit.

Low overheads have helped nurture an innovative start-up scene where founders can take a punt on a new venture without wagering a vast amount of capital. It also doesn't hurt that Vietnam is one of Asia's fastest-growing economies and Ho Chi Minh City is its financial capital. It's a particularly lucrative destination for those looking to make the most of the country's position as a major hub for high-tech manufacturing, especially in the technology sector (Intel and Samsung have already heavily invested in assembly sites). The city is also home to the country's largest airport, from which it's easy to make the most of its position at the crossroads of southeast Asia with an abundance of quick connections across the region.

Key facts:

Population: 8.8 million	

Key trades: Finance, logistics, tourism, healthcare, and education

Time it takes to register a new business: 1 month

Closest airport: Ho Chi Minh City's Tan Son Nhat International Airport has non-stop passenger flights to 49 destinations in 20 different countries, plus 19 domestic routes

Average wage: €3.50/hour

Cost of a beer: €0.80

Hours of sunlight per year: 2,299

USA
Boulder
The plucky Colorado city that punches above its weight

It's worth rising early in Boulder to drive the short distance to the start of the Chautauqua Trail. As the sun comes up you can take in vistas of the city and the breathtaking Flatirons (jagged rockfaces that dominate the scenery). If any proof were needed of the quality of life in the city nestled in a valley near the Rockies, you can find it here.

Boulderites are an outdoor tribe. The 1960s and 1970s were key decades, when the "elders" (as those still alive today are called) established environmental rules such as a maximum building elevation of 55ft (16.8 metres) – the rough height of a cottonwood tree. It was around then that Boulderites voted to tax themselves to fund land acquisition and the city owns and manages more than 18,000 hectares of parkland. Meanwhile the neat centre offers restaurants that wouldn't look out of place in major metropolises.

Almost all native and adoptive Boulderites say the sense of community and talent pool were decisive factors in staying. Boulder is home to 17 federally funded labs, a large University of Colorado campus, renowned advertising firm Crispin Porter Bogusky and design and consultancy firm Stantec Vibe.

Key facts:

Population: 326,196

Key trades: Aerospace, bioscience, outdoor recreation

Time it takes to register a new business: 2 to 3 days

Closest airport: Denver International Airport (45-minute drive) has non-stop passenger flights to 216 destinations in 13 countries, plus 190 domestic routes

Average wage: €27/hour

Average property price: €591,300

Cost of a beer: €5

Hours of sunlight per year: 3,100

Leipzig
The small-scale city that packs a punch when it comes to creative credentials

Pint-sized Leipzig is a fast-growing city. This is thanks not only to the presence of big-name businesses such as Porsche and BMW but also the magnetism of its relaxed, free-thinking atmosphere. Following the fall of the Iron Curtain, Leipzig – an industrial centre in the days of GDR – was filled with empty warehouses that were quickly infiltrated by artists and squatters looking to live on the cheap. In the mid-2000s students graduating from the city's renowned art school also started making Leipzig their permanent home rather than fleeing to Germany's bigger cities. This, in turn, helped shape a liberal atmosphere and set up some of the city's many galleries and music venues.

Today it remains a haven for young creatives, with much more affordable rental prices than Berlin. The city is also easier on the eye than the German capital, which is only an hour's train ride away. As a trade-fair town (or Messestadt) the East German city also draws thousands of visitors each year with its impressive roster of international events, including the celebrated Leipzig Book Fair and vast Leipzig Auto Show.

Key facts:

Population: 591,000

Key trades: Auto industry and suppliers, healthcare and biotech, energy and environment, media and creative industries

Time it takes to register a new business: 2 weeks

Closest airport: Leipzig/Halle Airport has non-stop passenger flights to 19 international destinations in 7 countries, plus 5 domestic routes

Cost of a beer: €3.50

Hours of sunlight per year: 1,502

Find your patch —— Where to set up

PORTUGAL
Ericeira
The coastal haven where entrepreneurs are making waves – and surfing them

The former fishing hamlet of Ericeira, about 50km north along the coast from Lisbon, is a surfing mecca, famed for its consistently high-quality waves. But recently it has been attracting more than just surfing types and weekenders, with increasing numbers of entrepreneurs choosing the laidback town as the perfect base for both raising a family and starting a business.

In 2015 the town hall inaugurated the small incubator Ericeira Business Factory. One of its start-ups is Sponsh, which tackles water shortages by capturing air vapour. "I manage to surf twice a week and if I need to travel, I'm only a 30-minute drive from Lisbon airport," says founder Lourens Boot.

There are also a handful of handy co-working spaces in the town, including Salt Studio which was founded by Mariana Ricciardi who opted out of her small Lisbon apartment to try life by the sea. "When I arrived, I was working as a freelancer and it was impossible to find anywhere decent to work from," she says. "I thought that if I'm having this problem, others must be too." Shortly after opening the site she was managing a waiting list of mostly northern Europeans in dire need of a desk and a sense of community.

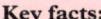

Key facts:

Population: 10,260	
Key trades: Tourism (surfing)	
Time it takes to register a new business: 7 days	
Closest airport: Lisbon Portela Airport (30-minute drive) has non-stop passenger flights to 145 destinations in 52 countries, plus 9 domestic routes	
Cost of a beer: €1.50	
Hours of sunlight per year: 2,801	

East Neuk, Fife

The foodie idyll bringing talent to
Scottish shores

With the North Sea on three sides, East Neuk takes its name from the old Scot word meaning "corner" and consists of a clutch of small fishing towns and farming settlements. A 40-minute drive south of Dundee, the area is unusually fertile due to the twin blessings of volcanic soil and a warm (for Scotland) microclimate and is famous for its food, including langoustines, oats and potatoes.

"Food and pride are so inextricable, particularly in rural communities," says Toby Anstruther, co-founder of Food from Fife, a network that brings together and promotes the area's producers. Anstruther has also repurposed some of the region's former farm steadings as studio spaces. Here the remit of businesses goes further than just food: there are graphic designers, a guitar and mandolin-maker, a photographer and a stained-glass-window designer, among other people.

Everyone on site agrees that coming together has made their businesses greater than the sum of their parts. "Many of us were kitchen-table set-ups," says Kirsty Thomas of studio Tom Pigeon, whose clients have included some of London's great cultural institutions, not least the V&A and the Tate. "It's not just about having more space to grow our businesses – we all feed off the sense of community here."

Find your patch —— Where to set up

Key facts:

Population: 374,000
Key trades: Energy and renewables, fintech, food and drink
Time it takes to register a new business: 24 hours
Closest airport: Edinburgh Airport (1-hour drive) has non-stop passenger flights to 139 destinations in 37 countries, plus 18 domestic routes
Average wage: €13.60/hour
Average property price: €203,885
Cost of a beer: €4.65
Hours of sunlight per year: 1,430

Kingston, Ulster County
The rural outpost drawing urbanites from the Big Apple

Moving Upstate for cheaper property and more space is not uncommon for New Yorkers; Hudson in Columbia County, accessible by train from Penn Station, has been evolving into a mini Brooklyn for years. But on the other side of the river in Ulster County, a small city is bubbling with activity. In Kingston, which has no train link to New York, a wave of scrappy entrepreneurs are creating a vibrant community.

While many transplants bring their professions with them, others find new ones. Musicians Mark Palmer and Anthea White moved Upstate from Brooklyn in 2017 and opened Village Coffee and Goods in Kingston, a café that stocks locally made products. "We felt like there was something special happening here," says White. Twenty miles southwest of Kingston, Italian photographer Fabio Chizzola bought the abandoned Westwind Orchard as a weekend escape and ended up running a farm, restaurant, cidery and shop. Visit on a warm evening – as locals laze on blankets on a sweeping green lawn chatting over bottles of cider and crispy pizzas – and you'll soon grasp the appeal of moving to Ulster County.

Key facts:

Population: 23,000
Key trades: Food and drink, business, arts
Time it takes to register a new business: 7 days
Closest airport: LaGuardia Airport (90-minute drive) has non-stop passenger flights to 84 destinations in 5 countries, plus 78 domestic routes
Average property price: €270,700
Cost of a beer: €4.20
Hours of sunlight per year: 2,656

Find your patch —— Where to set up

FRANCE

Guéthary

The Basque beach town filling with creative talent

When travelling down the Basque coast from Biarritz to San Sebastián, you could easily miss Guéthary. This former fishing village perched atop a rocky cliff is not like neighbouring seaside resorts. "There are no discos, no champagne bars and no soap shops here," says Antoine Piechaud who runs café and event space Providence with his wife Caroline. "Guéthary is a bit of a bubble of its own."

With roaring waves a five-minute walk down the road, life in Guéthary beats to a laidback rhythm that's typical of surfing spots. "Years ago, people working in fields such as design, music or fashion realised that they could live, work and surf from here year-round," says Piechaud. As a music industry professional, he was one of them: Piechaud relocated from Paris, drawn by the promise of a slower pace of life amid a tight-knit community.

Another resident is Swedish-born ceramicist Lena Baltazard who moved to the Basque coast 20 years ago, when she bought her light-filled atelier-boutique. From here, she throws cups and other tableware for private clients and restaurateurs, such as Providence. "In many other places, I'd be stuck in traffic jams on a daily basis," says Baltazard, "here, I can use that time to go swimming in the sea instead."

Key facts:

Population: 1,327	

Key trades: Real estate, manufacturing

Time it takes to register a new business: 2 weeks

Closest airports: Biarritz airport (20-minute drive) has non-stop passenger flights to 20 destinations in 8 countries, plus 9 domestic routes

Average wage: €13/hour

Average property price: €519,700

Cost of a beer: €5

Hours of sunlight per year: 2,089

AUSTRALIA
King Valley
The verdant valley where crops and businesses grow side-by-side

A three-hour drive northeast of Melbourne, Victoria's King Valley is a bucolic region of dairy farms, vineyards, nut-producing smallholdings and a burgeoning tourism sector. Once an epicentre of Australia's tobacco industry, the region now resembles a gumtree-flecked Tuscany, replete with cypress trees, lush green hills and patches of yellow fields.

Comprising a cluster of villages set among rolling hills, the King Valley was settled in the postwar period by Italian immigrants lured by the availability of agriculture jobs. Many stayed. Now the region is home to about 35 wine producers, growing Italian varieties such as nebbiolo, sangiovese and prosecco. There's also a prominent dairy industry centred on the township of Milawa, along with farms rearing beef cattle and goats, and growing nuts.

King Valley holds plenty of appeal to would-be "tree changers" (as Australians call urbanites leaving for rural outposts) hoping to set up a business. A combination of fertile land and plenty of rainfall helps. There's also a co-operative, close-knit community and affordable land prices. "It used to be a secret but people are starting to find out about it here," says King Valley entrepreneur Alan Tainton, who runs a small, upscale accommodation offering with his wife Rowena called 3 Black Sheds.

Key facts:

Population: 1,890
Key trades: Wine, agriculture and cattle farming
Time it takes to register a new business: 2 days
Closest airport: Albury Airport has 4 domestic flights; Melbourne airport (3 hour drive) has non-stop passenger flights to 59 destinations in 19 countries, plus 31 domestic routes
Average wage: €16/hour
Average property price: €412,269
Cost of a beer: €4
Hours of sunlight per year: 3,031

PART 3.

100 SUCCESS STORIES

Have you ever wondered what life might be like if you took control of your career? Not by heading a multinational necessarily but maybe something more rewarding. Perhaps a long-dreamed-of B&B in the Alps or an eco-conscious fashion brand in a city where you can see the sea? While not everyone will (or for that matter *needs* to) change the world, it's enjoyable to imagine how a shift in vocation could pay dividends and makes things better for your surroundings at the same time.

A smart venture can also cause wider ripples too. Might your independent shop help revive the local high-street, fuel partner businesses nearby and provide others with meaningful work, places to linger and a better environment in which to work? Here's hoping.

Our selection of 100 businesses to benchmark is a rundown of operators large and small who made a simple decision. To start up and do things their own way – from the pay-for-entry bookshop in Japan and the beer-brewing trio in New Zealand to the South African curators who set up an art gallery in their home. So forget the idea that what you do is measured solely by income or turnover – this is what success can look like.

I.

Mmcité
Bílovice, Czech Republic

The street furniture-maker that created a new benchmark for public spaces

Founded: 1994
Employees: 250
Annual turnover: €29m

From its base and production facilities in the Czech Republic (sustainable new premises are being built in South Moravia in addition to the current HQ in Bílovice), Mmcité has supplied benches and other street furniture to over 30 countries worldwide. Even before the 2013 commission to make bus-stop shelters at Paris's Charles de Gaulle Airport that bolstered its international image, the street-furniture manufacturer had always put the emphasis on improving public space. "Good design can have a positive impact on behaviour," explains David Karasek, owner of Mmcité (*pictured*). "If there is poor-quality design on the street, people feel they're being treated negatively."

With branches in other European countries and in the US, the company mainly employs homegrown Czech talent but it has also worked with international designers. It previously collaborated with landscape architect James Corner (famed for his work on New York's High Line) on a park designed for Philadelphia's Navy Yard.

Q&A with David Karasek

1. **How did you come up with the idea?** It was obvious to me: public space just screamed out for better quality of function and aesthetics, so street furniture seemed to be the right way to go.
2. **What's the biggest challenge of your sector?** The top challenge for designers in general is to develop products that are well balanced functionally, aesthetically and economically.
3. **How did you secure funding?** We funded our development and manufacturing from the profits that we made – old school.
4. **What's the best thing about being your own boss?** Freedom. And having people who admire you every day.

2.

Studio Astolfi
Lisbon

The visual merchandiser elegantly illuminating window displays

Founded: 2007
Employees: 15
Became profitable after: 5 years

There's no doubt that window displays are an art form, and one of the finest examples is Portugal's Studio Astolfi, which has carved an attractive niche for brands including Hermès. Studio Astolfi's work for the famed luxury goods purveyor has wowed the passersby of its shops in Portugal, Spain and France, where objects and spaces mesmerise customers.

The woman behind the studio is architect and designer Joana Astolfi, who founded her company in 2007, combining her training with a passion for the visual arts and collecting secondhand objects. While she started solo by doing individual projects and collaborations, today the studio relies on a small staff comprising artists and architects, as well as an external team of woodcarvers, welders and glassmakers to turn her vision into reality – her imaginative commissions can take anything from two months to two years to complete. "Window displays are a sort of open-air gallery," says Astolfi.

Q&A with Joana Astolfi

1. **What advice would you have given to yourself at the beginning?** To develop my business skills earlier. I'm a creative person but as the founder of the studio I need to be fully involved in the business side of things too. I now have a team that helps me but there were some early projects where we ended up making a loss because I didn't present more realistic fees.

2. **How do you build your team?** I'm not interested in portfolios and CVs, I like to meet people. I want to find out what their passion is and why they love what they're doing. They don't need to know it all, in fact I like when new team members grow while they work at the studio.

3.

Tiipoi
London / Bangalore

The homeware brand updating Indian crafting traditions

Founded: 2013
Employees: 16
Became profitable after: 5 years

Spandana Gopal's design brand Tiipoi was born out of a frustration with the stereotypes surrounding Indian craftsmanship. After leaving her native Bangalore to study in London, Gopal became aware of how old-fashioned crafting techniques were often romanticised by consumers. "I wanted to create handcrafted products that were more functional and less like souvenirs," she says.

She enlisted designer Andre Pereira to develop a range including brass candleholders, glass jars and stainless-steel teapots, all made by the brand's team of craftspeople in Bangalore. "We try to keep as much as possible in-house because it gives us a lot of control over the quality and the working conditions," says Pereira. "We have two master craftsmen (a metal spinner and ceramicist) who each have a team under them." Tiipoi has expanded its offering to include colourful home textiles, vases modelled on Bangalore's brutalist structures and traditional Longpi ceramic cookware.

Q&A with Spandana Gopal and Andre Pereira

1. **How did you come up with the idea?** I kept thinking, why isn't there an Indian version of Muji? There are a lot of stereotypes around Indian craft and a lot of it is based around nostalgia. A lot of designers are thinking more about how they can prolong these crafting traditions rather than develop them in a sustainable way.

2. **What's the biggest challenge of your sector?** There's a big yes culture when it comes to manufacturing in India – people will tell you they can make something without having the know-how so you really have to explain what you want. At the start we had to push to visit manufacturers' facilities to see what they could actually do.

4.

Ambientec
Yokohama, Japan

The illumination experts providing the lowdown on soft lighting

Founded: 2009
Employees: 14
Annual turnover: €1.5m to €2.3m

Yoshinori Kuno is the CEO of Ambientec, a small Japanese company that specialises in cordless home lighting. Kuno was renowned for his award-winning underwater-camera lighting and when he decided to adapt the technology to the domestic sphere, he looked for a designer who could translate his ideas. That man was Ryuichi Kozeki (*pictured, on right, with Kuno*), designer of Ambientec's first light: Bottled, a portable glass lamp with four brightness settings. "Japanese rooms tend to be bright whereas I want to make rooms as dark as possible," says Kuno.

With Xtal, the second light, Kuno wanted "the feel of a candle without making a fake candle" and chose to use crystal instead of cheaper acrylic. Today he also works with New York-based designer Nao Tamura and has reissued Samba-M, the wine-glass lamp by the late design legend Shiro Kuramata. Ambientec's Yokohama headquarters serves as a showroom, office and research studio, where the engineers test the products.

Q&A with Yoshinori Kuno

1. **What's the biggest challenge of your sector?** In postwar Japan the preference has been for bright lighting whether at home or on the high street. I like cosy, soft lighting but the majority still think the former is the better.
2. **What mistakes have you made and what have you learnt from them?** If you're wholehearted about a decision, you can learn a lesson and move forward even if it doesn't work out, but if you pursue something you're not 100 per cent sure about and it fails, then you'll be left with regret.
3. **What's the best thing about being your own boss?** I can stay true to myself, my own values and sensibility.

5.
The Ninevites
Stockholm / South Africa

The designer on a mission to keep traditional crafts alive

Founded: 2012 (registered 2016)
Employees: 1 (plus collaborators)
Annual turnover: €53,500

Nkuli Mlangeni-Berg's textiles brand The Ninevites was born during her time studying at Kaospilot, Denmark's alternative business school. While there, a research project took her to Peru where she met master weaver Mario Quispe who helped her produce prototype designs woven from local sheep's wool. Mlangeni-Berg worked with Girona's Studio Carreras on the initial collection to produce bold, geometric designs inspired by Zimbabwean Ndebele patterns and Kuba textiles from the Democratic Republic of Congo. These are transposed onto the brand's range of rugs, throws and cushions.

Quispe still produces some of the brand's designs from his home in Lima but Mlangeni-Berg has also expanded production to her native South Africa where she has enlisted female artisans in remote areas, who weave her rugs using locally sourced mohair. "In South Africa a lot of indigenous craft is dying out," says Mlangeni-Berg. "I'm trying to make more people excited about passing these skills onto the next generation."

Q&A with Nkuli Mlangeni-Berg
1. **How did you come up with the idea?** I come from a very colourful place with great stories and wonderful people, but I never saw any of that reflected in the magazines I bought or fashion shoots I saw. So I wanted to create a space for that – a space for my people.
2. **What advice would you have given yourself at the beginning?** Be better at costing out your product, work on your prioritising and don't compare yourself to others.
3. **How do you choose your collaborators?** I mostly work with people who have a different skill set to mine; people with similar values and those I admire and respect.

6.

Studio Haos
Paris

The creative duo taking the plunge into the world of furniture

Founded: 2017
Employees: 5
From idea to reality: 18 months

In 2017, Sophie Gelinet was growing frustrated with her graphic design studio and her clients' demands. Her partner Cédric Gepner, an entrepreneur with a passion for design, suggested that she start making objects instead. "I told her, 'People will either like it or they won't but you'll get to make it exactly the way you want to'," says Gepner. What followed was Studio Haos, founded by the couple in Paris.

    They started with a ceramic, brass and blown-glass table lamp, which quickly became a success. When orders started pouring in from New York to Tokyo, they quit their jobs to devote themselves to a whole collection. Their portfolio now includes a bench, floor lamp, coffee table, armchairs and wall lights, all produced with the long-term in mind. Remarkably, neither of them have any formal design training. "Paradoxically, not being an expert and not knowing all the constraints associated with each material gives us more creative freedom," adds Gepner.

Q&A with Cédric Gepner

1. **What advice would you have given yourself at the beginning?** Have confidence in what you're creating. The hard part of design is not finding inspiration because there's so much of it out there. The difficulty lies in filtering it down, finding the best and not being intimidated by it.

2. **What's the best thing about being your own boss?** The freedom to move around. Our team and studio are in Paris but we've recently spent months living in Tangier working with local craftsmen. We're currently in Lisbon.

3. **How do you build your team?** We look for people with the right kind of spirit and who work well with one another.

7.

Midgard
Hamburg

The design buffs who revived a historic lighting brand

Founded: 1919 / 2015
Employees: 10
Became profitable after: 5 years

David Einsiedler and partner Joke Rasch took over German lighting firm Midgard in 2015. The company was established by Curt Fischer in 1919 and the couple were avid collectors of its lamps, which they often sold in their Hamburg-based vintage design shop Ply. When they heard that the business was faltering, they approached Fischer's descendants who agreed to sell the brand complete with all rights, patents, archival documents, stock, machinery and tools.

Midgard lamps have been back in production since 2017 and two of its original modular lighting systems have been reissued: the 500 and 550 series based on the adjustable lamps that once furnished the Bauhaus school, and the Federzugleuchte, a spring-balanced lamp from the 1950s. The most recent addition to their catalogue is the sleek Stefan Diez-designed Ayno lighting system which is made entirely from recycled and recyclable materials, and can be easily repaired without any tools.

Q&A with David Einsiedler

1. **How did you come up with the idea?** Since my teens, I've been part of a Lambretta scooter club. In 1999, I built a workshop for the club and went to a flea market to find some lamps to kit it out. That was the first time I encountered Midgard and my interest stemmed from there.
2. **What advice would you have given yourself at the beginning?** It's not just about making a beautiful product, you need to think about how you're going to sell it too.
3. **What are the benefits of being based in Hamburg?** As a port city, Hamburg is really well-positioned for a company like ours that produces in Germany and ships worldwide.

8.

Maton Guitars
Melbourne

The guitar-makers who prioritise long-lasting relationships

Founded: 1946
Employees: 75
Annual turnover: €12.7m

The director of Melbourne's Maton Guitars, Linda Kitchen, is proud that the company her father founded back in the 1940s now exports to China and Russia but vows it will never manufacture overseas. As the firm expands, Kitchen is determined it will continue to build its instruments in Australia despite the higher costs of production. "We're a handmade quality product," says Kitchen, who owns the company with her husband Neville. "If we move away from where we started, we lose our soul."

   Since Kitchen's father, Bill May, began selling guitars that he made in his backyard, these acoustic and electric instruments have been embraced by famous Australian performers, including Tommy Emmanuel and singer-songwriter Paul Kelly. Elvis Presley strummed a Maton in the 1957 film *Jailhouse Rock* while the brand's electric guitar that was played by George Harrison in 1963 fetched $485,000 (€445,000) at auction. Today, the company produces 8,000 guitars each year.

Q&A with head of marketing, Mark Mansour
1. **Who founded the business and why?** Bill May was a woodwork teacher and a musician. The difficulty in procuring good quality instruments after the war led him to make his own. The first guitar still hangs in our offices.
2. **What are the biggest challenges of your sector?** Finding skilled labour, sourcing sustainable timbers and supply chain.
3. **What does company culture mean to you?** Building a company around a set of values. We have relationships with suppliers that have lasted generations which I believe is fitting as the instruments we create are often passed down from one generation to the next as well.

9.
Nada Debs
Beirut

The interiors designer proving it pays to experiment

Founded: 2005
Employees: 16
Annual turnover: €2.5m

When Nada Debs moved to Beirut in 2000, she discovered a distinct lack of locally made furniture that honoured the area's rich craft heritage. The Lebanese designer, who grew up in Japan where her family ran a textiles business, set about filling this gap with a new aesthetic where clean lines and extravagant patterns collide. "I decided to look at the region's beautiful craftwork and apply it to more contemporary forms. My furniture gave me the answer to my identity crisis, which was torn between Japanese and Arab cultures," says Debs.

The company's studio is housed in a large 1930s mansion block in Beirut's Gemmayze neighbourhood. The typical Lebanese building – complete with Carrara marble flooring and terrazzo tiles – is the perfect foil to the brand's unique look. "Designing furniture has shown me that you can apply two opposing elements and the hybrid will work. I want to continue pushing the boundaries of craft in my region," says Debs.

Q&A with Nada Debs

1. **How did you come up with the idea?** By the time I had moved to Beirut, my work was instilled with the importance of heritage in design. I was curious about Middle Eastern craft and decided to experiment with it – ultimately it created a new identity in Arab design which I call Neo-Arabian.
2. **What are the benefits of being based in Beirut?** The accessibility to quality craftspeople in the area and the willingness to experiment.
3. **What's the biggest challenge of your sector?** The skills involved in traditional Lebanese furniture-making are a dying craft, so we must bring the craftspeople work to keep it going.

10.

Turbo
Amman

The graphic designers igniting Jordan's creative scene

Founded: 2015
Employees: 2
Initial capital: €14,000

In a refurbished split-level shop in downtown Amman you'll find Turbo's headquarters. The small but ambitious design and branding agency was founded in 2015 by graphic designers Saeed Abu-Jaber and Mothanna Hussein after their paths crossed in Beirut. "We were both big fans of the poster medium and we liked each other's work, so we decided to partner up," says Abu-Jaber.

The pair have created a look that has both international appeal and a strong Middle Eastern flavour: the walls of the contemporary office are imprinted with Turbo's logo, which makes use of the beautiful Arabic letter form. But its offering goes beyond simply branding – while the mezzanine is used for the agency's design work, the ground level is where it hosts a range of events from exhibitions and print sales to workshops and lectures. "The space has given us the opportunity to expand on what a design studio can be," says Abu-Jaber. "We wanted it to play a part in the cultural scene of the city."

Q&A with Turbo founders

1. **How did you come up with the idea?** We knew we wanted to partner up and start a design studio or space – we found two garages in Downtown Amman which gave us the opportunity to expand.
2. **What are the benefits of being based in Amman?** First of all, we both grew up here and it is home to us. Also, small design studios are quite scarce in the city so we knew there was a gap in the market.
3. **What is the best thing about being your own boss?** The general flexibility and the freedom to choose how to deal with certain situations, such as how to communicate with a client and how to go about a project.

II.

Fabien Cappello
Guadalajara

The designer who switched continents to find new inspiration

Founded: 2010
Employees: 4
Became profitable after: 2 years

French designer Fabien Cappello studied at Switzerland's illustrious ÉCAL University before setting up his eponymous studio in London in 2010. After six years in the British capital, he decided it was time to try somewhere new. "I was turning 30 and wanted to be somewhere that would allow me more space for reflection," says Cappello. "After visiting friends in Mexico I decided that's where I wanted to be. So I booked a one-way ticket."

Capello started afresh in Mexico City where he worked for four years on everything from woven loungers for Mexa Design to custom furniture for the city's Archivo Library. Today he retains a small studio in Mexico City but he was drawn to move his main practice to Guadalajara by its rich heritage of manufacturing and craft. "Even before I moved to Guadalajara, I was coming here often to produce my work," says Cappello. "The city has lots of amazing artisanal workshops. I find it more interesting to be here than in a design capital."

Q&A with Fabien Cappello
1. **What advice would you give yourself at the beginning?** Do things exactly how you feel like doing them, take your time, never accept compromises that you don't feel comfortable with and don't stress about your visibility on social networks. Keep yourself busy but never try to be what you are not.
2. **What are the benefits of being based in Guadalajara?** It is a city of production – there are a lot of interesting factories, fascinating workshops and potential resources for production. It is a really engaging place to produce projects.
3. **How did you build your team?** They were all close collaborators and they've become friends.

12.

Arch & Hook
Amsterdam

**The eco-hanger brand thinking small
to create big change**

Founded: 2015
Employees: 50
Annual turnover: €82.5m

Sustainability is all about small changes done at scale and in the retail world, there's one little but indispensable item that has long been ripe for a rethink. "We thought, 'hangers are everywhere, why are these not being looked at?'" says Sjoerd Fauser, CEO and founder of Dutch hanger brand Arch & Hook. "Of around one billion plastic hangers [in the UK], only 5 per cent are being recycled every year. That's horrendous."

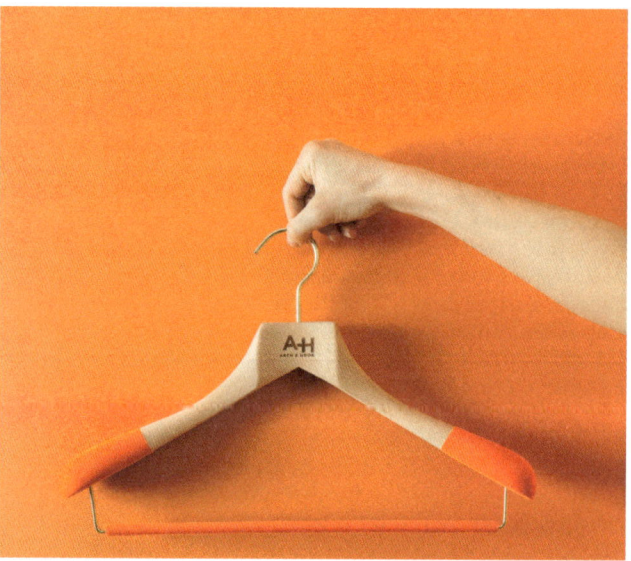

Since launching the first ever customisable wooden hanger to be made entirely from FSC-approved forests in 2016, the firm has won contracts with companies ranging from Levi's to Selfridges and Soulcycle. Realising how much demand there was for long-lasting, well-designed hangers, the brand added two plastic versions – both 100 per cent recycled and recyclable, and made from marine-waste material. Arch & Hook has since expanded internationally and is now moving into sustainable materials for other products, including packaging, furniture and fixtures.

Q&A with Sjoerd Fauser

1. **How did you secure funding?** After 100 people said no, a large Dutch family office believed in our vision. It's important to have a solid relationship between entrepreneur and investor and it's something that I work very hard to maintain.
2. **What's the biggest challenge of your sector?** Sustainability is on almost every organisation's agenda, yet change regarding plastic consumption is not happening – and certainly not at the necessary scale and speed.
3. **What's the best thing about being your own boss?** Having the freedom to build a team of enlightened and inspiring people and explore new ways to give back to our planet.

13.

Iperborea
Milan

The publisher taking a novel approach to stand out from the crowd

Founded: 1987
Employees: 13
Books released each year: 30+

Milan-based publishing house Iperborea has long been committed to introducing Italian readers to authors from northern Europe. The business is now headed by Pietro Biancardi but it was founded by his mother Emilia Lodigiani in 1987. She discovered her passion for Nordic literature while living in Paris. Here, she realised many titles weren't available back home. Today, the publishing house prints more than 30 titles each year.

Since taking over, Biancardi has introduced a number of ploys to attract bookshop browsers: he commissions eye-catching designs and plays around with book formats – for example, shrinking the size of a novel to a skinny 10cm by 20cm. "It fits in the back pocket of your jeans like an iPhone," he says. Expanding its collection beyond Nordic reads, Iperborea has launched 'The Passenger' – a series of travel guides containing long-form essays, articles and infographics, now translated into multiple languages. "People want to explore and they want to do it via print," he says.

Q&A with Pietro Biancardi

1. **How did your mother come up with the idea?** When she lived in Paris she discovered many Nordic authors that were unknown in Italy. She fell in love with their works and so she decided to bring them home.
2. **What's the biggest challenge of your sector?** In Italy, there are over 70,000 new books released every year, so you need to create a product that is instantly recognisable.
3. **What advice would you have given yourself at the beginning?** It's not enough to just print beautiful books, you have to sell them. So make sure you have a member of your team dedicated specifically to that.

14.

L'Étiquette
Paris

The menswear magazine subscribing to a new way of thinking

Founded: 2018
Employees: 3-6
Annual turnover: €1m

L'Étiquette proposes a refreshingly accessible vision for what men want to wear. Backed by So Press, an independent Parisian publisher, this collaborative "punk" project is by some of Paris's leading creative talents, including journalist Marc Beaugé, designer and vintage dealer Gauthier Borsarello and famed creative director Franck Durand (*pictured, l-r*). Unlike the majority of fashion publications, filled with head-to-toe new-season looks, this biannual magazine features a mix of well-worn and new-season items from brands high and low.

Shoots are complemented with factual tidbits and features about clothing culture. "There aren't many magazines where guys can really say, 'That could be me, I could wear those clothes'," says Beaugé. *L'Étiquette*, by contrast, is "like your stylish friend giving you advice". Its world is expanding fast: in early 2021 the team launched an English edition and they're also doing a podcast and a newsletter; a website and retail venture are coming soon.

Q&A with Marc Beaugé

1. **How did you come up with the idea?** We all knew each other and were working individually on different projects. The key part was getting to work all together on one project. It came naturally. Everyone working on *L'Étiquette* shares a common vision on fashion.
2. **What's the biggest challenge of your sector?** Not selling your soul. Fashion magazines do it way too often to please brands and get advertisers. We want to put our readers first – that is the challenge.
3. **How do you build your team?** On instinct and through our network. We want people with skills *and* values – skills alone are not enough.

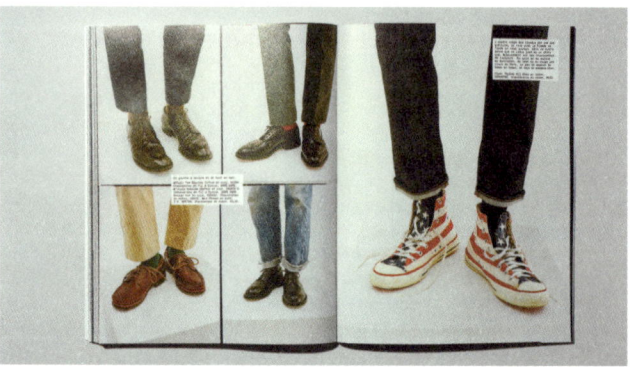

15.

The Big Bend Sentinel
Marfa, Texas

The newspaper with a perfectly blended business model

Founded: 2019 (originally 1926)
Employees: 22
Became profitable after: 18 months

Many publications have discovered that pairing a coffee shop with a print purveyor can do wonders for newsstands sales, but not many local newspapers have attempted this hybrid model. Enter the Texan-based weekly *The Big Bend Sentinel* and accompanying *Presidio International* where punters can enjoy a coffee in the heart of its headquarters.

Editor in chief Maisie Crow bought the Marfa-based titles with her husband Max Kabat in 2019. Crow has a background in journalism, while Kabat works in strategy consulting. "We realised we could combine our skill sets to reinvent the business model," says Kabat. Other than bolstering the paper's coffers, the new approach has opened up interesting editorial opportunities: the café serves as a gathering place that attracts ideas through osmosis. "It becomes an interesting place to exchange information," he says. The pairing is a natural fit: Crow and Kabat have found a way to offer economically sustainable local news – and the place to hear all about it.

Q&A with Max Kabat

1. **What's the biggest challenge of your sector?**
   The local, independent media business has been dying a slow death for two decades. We're trying to prove a path forward that's about quality not quantity. And the businesses – service and retail – that we chose to help support the running of the newspaper are labour and overhead-intensive.
2. **What does company culture mean to you?**
   As a strategy consultant you constantly preach its importance. Implementing it on your own brand is something else. It's the lifeblood of the business and we've worked hard to make it our top priority.
3. **The best thing about being based in Marfa?**
   It's a tight-knit community supportive of new ideas.

16.

NTS
London

The online radio station bringing together talent from around the world

Founded: 2011
Employees: 30
From idea to reality: 18 months

From Turkish psychedelia through to Russian techno and everything in between, NTS has made a name for itself by tapping into the world's most obscure and exciting music scenes. Every day, millions of global listeners tune in to discover the unexpected, and hear shows from the thousands of DJs and musicians who broadcast on the station's 12 online channels.

"There are only about three or four countries in the world where we don't have listeners," says CEO Sean McAuliffe, who joined founder Femi Adeyemi (*both pictured, Adeyemi on left*) in the station's early days. The enterprise has grown far beyond a simple platform for music streaming; it encompasses a record label, creative studio and a service called Space Tapes that curates background music for commercial buildings (their first client was New York's Rockefeller Centre). In 2020 NTS also set up a subscription service where listeners pay a small monthly fee to access special perks and support the station's ad-free model.

Q&A with Femi Adeyemi

1. **How did you come up with the idea?** The mainstream radio channels were very stuck on the commercial side and a lot of the pirate stuff just played the same kind of music. I wanted to create a platform that highlighted the diverse music tastes that me and a lot of my friends had.

2. **What was your initial capital?** I had £5,000 (€5,800) from a mix of savings and support from youth charity The Prince's Trust. It set me up with this great mentor. He didn't quite get what I was trying to do but he could see my passion.

3. **What advice would have given to yourself at the beginning?** Spend enough time not working – it will make your business better.

17.

QDY Magazine
Taipei

The passionate magazine publisher that speaks to the virtues of print

Founded: 2014
Employees: 8
Initial capital: €6,000

QDY Magazine (or *Qiudaoyu*) is an award-winning lifestyle magazine that covers Japan and Japanese culture from a Taiwanese perspective: the colourful quarterly is produced by a small team in Taipei and is written in Chinese. Each issue unpacks Japanese fashion, music, design, cuisine and travel for young Taiwanese. Most readers are aged between 20 and 35 and share a fascination with Japan.

   Editor in chief Eva Chen (*pictured, centre*), one of the title's founders, jumped into the magazine business straight out of university at an interesting time for the publishing industry. Around 2011, technology was eating away at traditional business models and creating opportunities for plucky independent publishers. After experimenting with a few ideas, Chen and her team settled on Japan as their editorial focus and within four years *QDY Magazine* was turning a profit and being lauded at Taiwan's annual publishing industry awards.

Q&A with Eva Chen
1. **How did you secure funding?** We were recent college graduates at the time and secured funds through online crowdfunding, advertising sponsorships and a youth entrepreneurship grant.
2. **What's the biggest challenge of your sector?** When we established *QDY* the publishing industry was at a turning point: consumers were looking for even more rapid and interactive information. In the face of this we try to emphasise the virtues of printed matter.
3. **What does company culture mean to you?** We are a team of just eight but we empower each member to create their own portfolio and encourage them to bring own way of working.

18.

Kolt
Olten, Switzerland

The journalist who forged a new media model that answers to the community

Founded: 2009
Employees: 7
Turnover: €275,000

Olten might not be Switzerland's media capital but it's still home to one of the country's most interesting journalistic models. *Kolt* was launched in 2009 as a culture magazine but in 2020 co-founder Yves Stuber decided to switch things up. *Kolt* was relaunched as a digital subscription that actively contributes to the community.

For €19 a month, subscribers become much more than readers: they can suggest newsworthy topics and rate whether other users' ideas should be pursued. "The instant response and active exchange with peers make the difference," says Stuber. But the team still recognises a need for a print edition and a gazette is now printed every fortnight. This paper version is distributed across local venues, as well as being posted directly to its subscribers. And there's an added touch: every subscriber receives a personalised greeting above the opener. "The print version allows people to discover stories that they might have scrolled past," he says. "In a way, we are closer to our local audience."

Q&A with Yves Stuber

1. **How did you secure funding?** Mainly from family and friends. We also had contributions from cultural funds, private benefactors and lots of personal time has been invested too.
2. **What advice would you have given yourself at the beginning?** Ask yourself what are your strengths? What are you good at and how do you do things? I'm good at connecting people to create amazing things that benefit a society.
3. **What are the benefits of being based in Olten?** It is basically the suburbs of Zürich, Bern, Basel and Lucerne. It is the perfect place to connect people. Plus the quality of life is very high at a comparatively lower cost.

19.

Vietcetera
Ho Chi Minh City

The expat entrepreneur who turned his curiosity into a business idea

Founded: 2016
Employees: 85
Annual turnover: €1.4m

Lifestyle-focused news site Vietcetera, published in both Vietnamese and English, is read by millions in a country where much of the media is state-controlled. "We are one of the few private media companies here and we happen to operate in a space where we need to be sensitive," says co-founder and CEO Hao Tran (*pictured, on left*). "But, given the kind of content we're creating, we're promoting Vietnam."

Tran is an overseas Vietnamese or "*Viet Kieu*". Originally from San Francisco he came back to the country that his parents left because of the Vietnam War. "My motivation for starting Vietcetera was to better understand Vietnam," he says. "My interest in media grew from discovery and learning about the industry." Today the site has the country well covered: from where to eat to what brands to own. While only a tiny fraction of readers visit the English site, it is a key portal for international brands looking to understand and invest in the rapidly developing country.

Q&A with Hao Tran

1. **What's the biggest challenge of your sector?** For the media industry at large, advertisers are still largely consumed by numbers, not the actual content.
2. **What advice would you have given yourself at the beginning?** Listen to your customers. In our case, our readers and clients. Document as much feedback as possible and share with your team.
3. **How long did it take to get from idea to reality?** Two years. The big milestone for us was adapting to the fact that we needed to be in Vietnamese, in addition to English. It was a difficult adjustment but proved necessary to bring the company up to the scale we enjoy today.

20.

Tajfuny
Warsaw

The travel journalist sharing her love of Asian literature

Founded: 2018
Employees: 9
Annual turnover: €380,000

Karolina Bednarz developed a deep interest in Asian literature and society, particularly Japan, while studying at university and later as a travel journalist. She discovered that she wasn't alone in her native Poland; there was a captive market for Asian titles translated into English or Polish. In 2018 she launched Tajfuny, a bookshop and publishing house that aims to broaden the horizons of Warsaw's literary scene.

The bookshop stocks a select list of 800 titles. Every book on display is loved by at least one member of staff. "Publishers send us books hoping we will stock them," says Bednarz. "But if they are not good enough, we won't." In fact, this notion extends into Tajfuny's publishing arm, where print quality is paramount – so far it has published 11 titles from Japan and Singapore. Its mission is to bring Asian literature to a western audience. "People who visit for the first time might be a bit lost but they return and ask for another book," says Bednarz.

Q&A with Karolina Bednarz

1. **What's the biggest challenge of your sector?** The constant price wars: we do not have a fixed book price system, so it is quite difficult for small publishers and independent bookstores to stay afloat. But we put a lot of energy into educating our readers why it is worth paying the cover price.
2. **What does company culture mean to you?** Our team is currently all women – we make most decisions together and everyone has a lot of independence regarding their responsibilities.
3. **How did you build your team?** Through open applications, asking questions about the applicants' fascination with Asia and books. And so far this human approach has worked very well.

21.

Live Magazine
Paris

The stage show where writers become performers

Founded: 2015
Employees: 5
Turnover: €900,000

Live Magazine is a performance that puts journalists, cartoonists and photographers centre stage at Parisian theatres. "We very rarely preview the programme and we never record anything," says founder Florence Martin-Kessler. "We want it to be like you're opening a magazine: you don't know what you're going to see. But there needs to be sadness, memoir, humour – and always a good story."

The former documentary maker came up with the idea while on a fellowship at Harvard. After meeting with Douglas McGray, who co-founded the similar *Pop-Up Magazine*, he suggested she bring the concept to Europe. Today, shows bring together 1,500-strong audiences who gather to hear everything from war reporters discussing life on the front line to more light-hearted fare, such as a woman who collects shopping lists. Theatre-goers pay upwards of €10 for a ticket and every performance is delivered with disarming intimacy, no script and few visual props.

Q&A with Florence Martin-Kessler

1. **How did you come up with the idea?** I had been studying journalism at Harvard as part of the Nieman scholarship program and at a reunion in 2013 I met Douglas McGray who was speaking on a panel about innovation in journalism.
2. **What's the best thing about being your own boss?** The freedom to choose who I work with.
3. **How do you build your team?** I rarely publish job listings. Most of the people I work with have just sent me their CV speculatively. If I see one I like, I'll try to meet them.
4. **What advice would you have given yourself at the beginning?** Don't wait.

22.

It's Freezing in LA
London

The independent magazine tackling climate change

Founded: 2018
From idea to reality in: 6 months
Annual turnover: €12,000 to €24,000

London-based magazine It's Freezing in LA was launched as a reaction against the uninspiring environmental journalism its editor Martha Dillon (*pictured, centre*) was tired of reading. She came together with graphic designer Matthew Lewis (*second from left*) and illustrator (and co-founder) Nina Carter (*second from right*) – now the magazine's creative directors – to make the publication. Their aim was to explore the subject in a more approachable way and appeal to people who wouldn't typically pick up a publication about the environment.

"We wanted to combine art and science and have a conversation between the two," says Dillon. "All our articles come from a different background. So you'll have a piece about law next to a piece about history, art or theatre." Today, alongside the bi-annual publication, the magazine organises talks, workshops and film screenings as well as recording its own podcast that has covered everything from guerilla gardening to politics and ecology in Lebanon.

Q&A with Martha Dillon
1. **How long until the business became profitable?** We broke even with issue two and profitability has varied since, but all profits go straight back into the following issues.
2. **How did you come up with the idea?** Our core team had backgrounds in climate activism, journalism and art. Having conversations across professions and fields felt like a rewarding way to push discourse about the environment forwards.
3. **What's the biggest challenge of your sector?** Accessibility – even when printed with recycled paper and run sustainably, magazines cost money to print and need transporting. This automatically makes them less accessible than a free website.

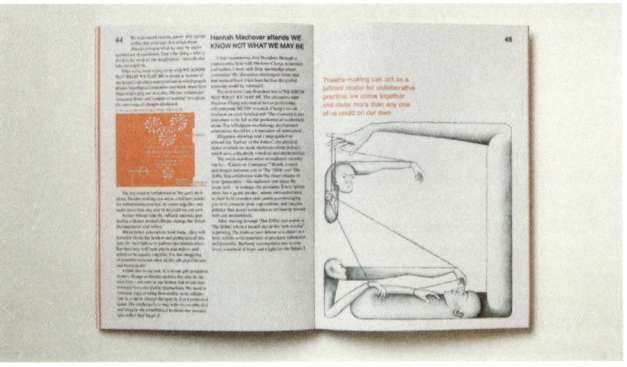

23.

The Greek Podcast Project
Athens

The journalist using podcasting to help grow Greece's independent media scene

Founded: 2020
Employees: 4
Initial capital: €8,000

Daphne Karnezis had been living in London for seven years when she decided to move back to her native Greece. After working as a journalist for the likes of Bloomberg and later in podcast production at MONOCLE, she saw an opportunity to take everything she'd learnt back to Athens. "I could see there was a lot of great young journalistic talent in the country but they often have few choices on where to work when it comes to young, independent media," says Karnezis.

Upon her return to Athens, she set up her own news and current affairs podcast which soon caught the eye of some of the country's biggest companies, who got in touch to ask her to help produce content for them. To meet demand, she assembled a team of journalists, sound designers and marketing experts to form the country's first dedicated podcast production company. *The Greek Podcast Project* has since collaborated with the likes of the Athens tourist board and international non-profit business incubator Endeavor.

Q&A with Daphne Karnezis

1. **What are the benefits of being based in Athens?** It's a great time to be here because of all the fresh talent that's returning to Greece after some tough years for the country. The podcast ecosystem is still young here, so it feels exciting to be part of that growth.
2. **How do you build your team?** Some of it is luck. You don't have to look for people in the exact same space but be prepared to do some training.
3. **What's the best thing about being your own boss?** The flexibility is great of course but it's also been a pleasure to welcome younger members to the team and feel like they're learning something from me.

24.

JNP Coffee
Bujumbura, Burundi

The entrepreneur bringing Burundi's coffee to the world stage

Founded: 2012
From idea to reality: 6 months to 1 year
Became profitable after: 3 years

With its nutrient-rich volcanic soil and high levels of rainfall, the small East African nation of Burundi boasts ideal climes for coffee growing. But despite being home to 600,000 growers producing high-quality beans, Jeanine Niyonzima couldn't understand why her native country wasn't getting the recognition it was due.

After giving birth to twins in 2012, she decided to step away from her high-flying corporate career in the US to help her cousin promote his Burundian coffee business. Through this, she noticed an opportunity to bring more growers to the global market. She founded JNP Coffee shortly after as a producer and exporter that helps farmers sell their beans to speciality roasters around the world. "A key part of the work is trying to empower farmers," says Niyonzima. Today, the business works with more than 2,000 growers at each of the three different wet mills in Burundi. "We make sure they're paid right and that their business is sustainable."

Q&A with Jeanine Niyonzima

1. **Why did you found JNP Coffee?** I was one of the very lucky ones – I was able to grow up and go to high school and get a chance to leave Burundi. Because of this, I felt a personal responsibility to give back to my country. For me, JNP Coffee was a means of empowering growers. It's a lot of work. But it's very personally rewarding.
2. **What advice would you have given yourself at the beginning?** If something isn't working then just cut it. Don't wait too long, it's OK to have a sunk cost. Having the right people with you is also key, so choose your team members carefully.

25.

Aeijst
Styria, Austria

**The Austrian gin brand that mixes
a foreign drink with local flavour**

Founded: 2014
Employees: 6
Annual turnover: €600,000

Though gin is mostly produced in the
UK, it enjoyed its first wave of popularity
in Austria during the postwar reconstruction
of the 1960s, when the country's economy
began to recover and Austrians could afford
imported drinks again. Today, thanks to
producers such as Wolfgang Thomann and
his family, they no longer need to import
it. Thomann's Aeijst distillery is one of two
dozen gin producers in the picturesque
province of Styria alone. Thomann says
that nostalgia for 1960s cocktails – such
as the gin fizz – played its part in fuelling
the tipple's boom, changing the image of
a drink that was once seen as being the
preserve of the elderly.

"Tastes have changed, even though gin
was late in arriving in Austria compared with
the UK or the US," says Thomann. Aeijst's
spirits are made from juniper (gin's core
ingredient) combined with other botanicals
such as lavender, ginger, coriander and
citrus zest, and can be found in the country's
best bars and specialist shops.

Q&A with Wolfgang Thomann
1. **What are the benefits of being based in
   Styria?** It is the perfect place to make gin.
   We are based in the middle of all the vineyards
   and the winemakers were happy to see something
   different, especially as we were the first distillery
   in the area. Now there are more than 20.
   South Styria is now known for its culinary
   delights, good wine and gin.
2. **What advice would you have given yourself
   at the beginning?** Stay true to yourself and
   don't follow every trend. Fast money is not
   always good money.
3. **How do you build your team?** That's easy: we
   are a family. Three generations of helping hands.

26.

Nãm
Lisbon

The entrepreneur turning someone's rubbish into something delicious

Founded: 2018
Employees: 6
Became profitable after: 3 years

Creating a business with a positive impact is not an easy task but for Natan Jacquemin this was the driving force that led to the creation of Nãm mushroom farm. Originally from Belgium, Jacquemin wanted to tap into Portugal's love affair with coffee and change the way we relate to food. He did this by using old coffee grounds to grow organic oyster mushrooms. The idea proved to be a success and caught the attention of Delta Cafés, Portugal's largest coffee roaster, which agreed to supply the grounds.

In 2020 Nãm moved into a new urban farm site: four shipping containers in Lisbon's Marvila neighbourhood were fitted to turn 3 tonnes of coffee grounds into fungi every month. And while 90 per cent of the fungi are sold to restaurants and markets, the urban farm also welcomes visitors. "It's not just the sustainability that attracts people, it's the quality too," says Jacquemin. "By being within the city, we're able to harvest in the morning and deliver in the afternoon."

Q&A with Natan Jacquemin
1. **How long did it take to get from initial idea to reality?** The first Nãm mushrooms were cultivated in my student dorm. From there, I found a small cave in the city centre and started growing at a very small scale. However it took around 2 years to get from the idea to the farm that exist today.
2. **How did you come up with the idea?** I have always dreamt of running my own company but I quickly realised that most businesses are not compatible with our planetary boundaries. I went on a hunt for a circular and sustainable business model that worked in terms of economy and ecology. It all started out of a need to do something concrete for our planet.

27.

Sunshine Juice
Tokyo

The juice-maker who scaled back his business when the time was ripe

Founded: 2014
Employees: 5 (full-time)
Initial capital: €67,000

Nori Ko says it was his grandfather's homemade pressed juices that sowed the seeds for his business. He'd be the first to admit that he had a lot to learn. At first, he was buying fruit and vegetables online and at local shops – he needs 1.5kg for each glass of juice – and the margins were tight. Once he got serious about the business, he built up a network of farmers, of which there are 20 today, and started buying directly.

With capital from a supportive investor, Sunshine Juice opened in 2014 and took off just as the juice boom was about to hit. In no time, Ko had 100 staff and several locations. But it wasn't the business he had in mind. He bought out the investor and scaled back to one location in Tokyo. "I was spending so much time travelling between shops and not getting outdoors, which is the part I like best." Since then, he's built up the online business and pursued more sustainable practices: he has switched from plastic to glass and sells a compost that he makes from discarded skins and husks.

Q&A with Nori Ko

1. **How did you come up with the idea?** I simply loved fresh juice. I was running a lot at that time and my body responded well to them. I thought it would be great to open a juice bar in Tokyo.
2. **How long did it take for the business to become profitable?** One year – there was definitely a boom for juice shops in 2015 and 2016!
3. **What's the biggest challenge of your sector?** Educating people about what we do and why our juice costs more than a drink from a corner store.
4. **What do you like most about being your own boss?** You can focus on what you really want to do, where you want to be and who you want to work with.

28.

Nordic Wasabi
Reykjavík

The crop-growers using new technology to spice up Iceland's exports

Founded: 2015
Employees: 5
From idea to reality: 2 years

Water quality is vital when growing wasabi. This is why engineer Ragnar Atli Tómasson chose the remote east of Iceland to cultivate the vegetable, using high-quality water filtered through volcanic rock. Most of what passes for wasabi in Europe is green paste made of mustard or horseradish which is then coloured with the stems. Tómasson grows his wasabi in greenhouses fitted with technology that alters brightness and humidity, mimicking the environment of the Japanese mountains where the crop originates.

Icelandic wasabi has become a neatly packaged souvenir for visitors: the fresh stem comes with an *oroshigane* (grater), for grinding the vegetable to a paste and a tiny bamboo brush for serving. With its main offices located in central Reykjavík, Tómasson invites passersby for daily tastings where he shares his knowledge of the crop. Today, the wasabi is flown to more than 100 restaurants across Europe, including the fêted Jordnaer in Copenhagen.

Q&A with Ragnar Atli Tómasson

1. **How did you come up with the idea?** We wanted to find a way to use the abundance of clean water and renewable electricity from hydroelectric resources here in Iceland, and to do something new and exciting. Wasabi is a high-end crop and there's demand in the market so we realised it was a feasible product to export.

2. **How do you consider your role on a local level?** We are discovering new ways to find markets for Icelandic products by selling directly to our customers. And we're the first ones to export vegetables in a country that mainly sells fish products – now local vegetable companies have started exporting to Denmark too.

29.

Garage Project
Wellington

The beer-brewers with a crafty idea and the ambition to keep experimenting

Founded: 2011
Employees: 90
Became profitable after: 2 years

In terms of consumption, Wellington has long been New Zealand's craft beer capital. But brothers Ian and Peter Gillespie and friend Jos Ruffell (*pictured, on right, with Ian*) often wondered why none of the beer being drunk in their hometown was actually being brewed there. To test the waters, they launched a small-scale pilot scheme in 2011 that produced 24 different beers in as many weeks. "We knew it wouldn't be commercially viable to brew in such small batches," says Ruffell, "but it allowed us to experiment and gauge interest."

The 24/24 project garnered so much momentum that it led the trio to set up a permanent base in a former petrol station (which gave the brewery its name) and by 2015 they were cited as being New Zealand's fastest growing company. Today, Garage Project releases more than 50 varieties each year. Ranging from Irish stouts to unfiltered lagers, the beers are packaged in eye-catching cans many of which are designed by local artists and illustrators.

Q&A with Jos Ruffell
1. **What advice would you have given to yourself at the beginning?** Think a bit further ahead. When we got to the end of the 24/24 project, we'd run out of money. We raised some cash from friends and other contacts and only then were we able to scale up. We didn't really think of growth beyond that – we were instantly chasing our tail and struggling to keep up.
2. **What do you like most about being your own boss?** Having an idea that you can follow all the way through. I used to work in video game development and the only feedback we'd get was numbers. It's amazing to be able to see people out there enjoying our beers.

30.

Le Relais de Castelet
Arles, France

The chef putting French classics back on the menu

Founded: 2015
Employees: 5
From idea to reality in: 1 year

"People know about us by word of mouth," says self-taught chef Jean-Baptiste Bert, founder of Le Relais du Castelet. "When we started hosting dinners here, we didn't even have a telephone." But Bert did have friends in the hospitality industry who helped him spread the word across Alpilles, east of Arles in Provence. The result is a true table d'hôte, where in-the-know food folk mix with chefs and sommeliers on their days off.

Bert and his two-person team have taken all the ambitious ingredients of running a restaurant – a daily changing menu, extensive wine list, on-point service – and distilled them into a relaxed, close-knit supper club. The food is rooted in Provençal family cooking, with staples including roasted game and *soupe au pistou*, all made using wild basil plucked from the 50-hectare site. "A lot of our guests keep coming back because hardly anyone is still cooking these dishes," says Bert with a hint of pride.

Q&A with Jean-Baptiste Bert

1. **How did you come up with the idea?** I decided to restore the hunting lodge on my family's land where hunters used to gather to eat together. We started using the space for private events which proved so successful we decided to become a proper restaurant.

2. **What's the biggest challenge of your sector?** The food and drink industry is competitive in Provence and very seasonal, so it's challenging to make a business profitable in the winter – you need a solid local client base.

3. **How do you build your team?** We're basically just friends who share the same passion for food and wine and have a keen attention to detail.

31.

Good to Gather
Stellenbosch, South Africa

The pop-up restaurant that became a permanent fixture

Founded: 2020
Employees: 6
From idea to reality: 2 weeks

Chef Jess Shepherd and her partner Luke Grant opened a pop-up restaurant at Rozendal, a biodynamic vinegar farm in Stellenbosch where Shepherd began her career 16 years ago as a short-term solution for increasing footfall to the farm. It has since become one of the hottest meal tickets in South Africa's Western Cape province.

Shepherd and Grant's former restaurant, The Table at De Meye, was known for lazy lunches on a sprawling lawn in the Cape Winelands. At their new location and under the name Good to Gather, the lunch and dinner series follows a similar set-up to their old haunt, serving a set menu of three family-style courses made from produce from independent farmers and their own garden. "There's a growing group of consumers who want to know where and how produce is grown," says Shepherd who has long advocated for small-scale producers and seasonal foods. Following the success of the pop-up restaurant, the couple intends to open a farm shop, also at Rozendal.

Q&A with Jess Shepherd and Luke Grant

1. **What advice would you have given yourself at the beginning?** Don't undervalue what you do.
2. **How do you build your team?** The members on our team have been working with us for a decade, through two previous businesses.
3. **What does company culture mean to you?** Work is such a large part of our lives, and we give up many hours that would be spent at home or with family. We decided when we started our first business that we would create an environment where everyone feels looked after: not only the customers but also our employees.
4. **What's the biggest challenge of your sector?** Being niche and finding your market.

32.

Las Vino
Margaret River, Australia

The young producer who forged his own path to create a full-bodied offering

Founded: 2013
Employees: 2 to 3
From idea to reality: 2 years

For Nic Peterkin, wine runs in the blood: his father is a winemaker and his mother hails from one of the area's oldest winemaking families. After applying to medical school, Peterkin surrendered to his fate and studied for a master's in oenology. He honed his skills in Mexico and the US before returning to Margaret River. "I had this burning desire to create the kind of wines that I'd tried overseas but by using different methods," he says. And so, in 2013, Las Vino was born.

While it's customary for producers to grow grapes onsite, Las Vino finds the best vineyards for each variety. "We use certain methods because they lead to wines that have more flavour," he says. In an industry that's defined by tradition, almost everything Peterkin does seems unconventional, be it buying grapes from other vineyards or producing different varietals, which are bottled in vessels that resemble champagne or port bottles. But Peterkin is fastidious when it comes to his craft. "I learnt from both sides of my family that the little things matter."

Q&A with Nic Peterkin
1. **What's the biggest challenge of your sector?** The variability of the weather – it takes part in how much you can produce and the quality. Some years our yield will be down by 50 per cent making it difficult to forecast cash flow.
2. **What does company culture mean to you?** Understanding what you and your staff value and working towards that together.
3. **How do you build your team?** If people like the vision you're projecting with the brand and business they will be drawn to work for or with your company.
4. **What's the best thing about being your own boss?** Surfing before work in the morning.

33.

Beard
Unzen, Japan

The small-scale restaurant that prioritises great produce above all else

Founded: 2021
Employees: 1
From idea to reality: 18 months

In Unzen, a little-known corner of Japan, talented chef Shinichiro Harakawa has shown how a single restaurant can lead a grass-roots movement. "Legendary farmer Masatoshi Iwasaki grows about 80 varieties of indigenous vegetables using organic and seed-saving methods," says Harakawa. "In the Unzen countryside, people were not yet interested in what he was doing. No local restaurant was using his vegetables, so I decided to open my own here."

Although Harakawa was running a popular restaurant in Tokyo, he left it to the co-owner and followed his passion, moving to the hot spring village of Obama in Unzen – population 7,700. He joined forces with Iwasaki and Chikashi Okutsu – who runs a direct-to-consumer organic vegetables shop in Unzen – and opened the eight-seat restaurant Beard in 2021 as a solo operation. This is a new chapter for Harakawa: sometimes it's hard to tell whether he's here to help the town, or the town has helped him to better understand his craft.

Q&A with Shinichiro Harakawa

1. **What are the benefits of being based somewhere rural?** I am able to keep running costs low. Although Unzen is a hot spring destination popular with tourists, there are no other restaurants like mine in the area.
2. **What's the biggest challenge of your sector?** Finding great staff. And providing a good working environment such as job security and a competitive salary.
3. **Any advice for those who want to start their own restaurant?** Try to create a high-quality small business. There is no need to borrow lots of money or do something beyond your ability. There are great opportunities in the countryside.

34.

Haven's Kitchen
New York

**The cooking teacher who discovered
a tasty solution for kitchen novices**

Founded: 2012
Employees: 8
Initial capital: €620,000

When Alison Cayne opened Haven's Kitchen cooking school and café, she "wanted a place where people could learn to feel confident about making dinner". Students knew the basics and wanted to make a meal from scratch but didn't fancy the time-consuming task of creating sauces. "They also didn't want to spend hours cleaning up," says Cayne. And thus the idea for high-quality prepared and packaged sauces was born.

Cayne began selling them from the café's fridge but soon garnered the attention of larger retailers. "It seemed like a product that helped people cook more," she says. Haven's Kitchen now creates six varieties and is gearing up to release more. But there is still work to do. "Consumers are unfamiliar with fresh sauce as a category," says Cayne. "They don't even know where to find it in a supermarket." Another challenge has been creating a product that is both high quality and accessible. "We don't want people to feel as though it's a special privilege to be able to buy our products."

Q&A with Alison Cayne

1. **How did you come up with the idea?** We looked at the sauce options on the market, and there was very little innovation: nothing was fresh, flavours were stale, and there was endless wasteful packaging. So we set out to change all of that.
2. **What advice would you have given yourself at the beginning?** Ask some fundamental questions: What are we making? Who are we making it for? Why are we making it? Who else is doing something similar and how do we compare?
3. **How do you build your team?** Like any ecosystem, diversity is key – in backgrounds, viewpoints and experiences. The more perspectives we have, the healthier I believe the business will be.

35.

Mercato Metropolitano
London

The plucky sustainable food market that's revitalising its neighbourhood

Founded: 2015
Employees: 60
Annual turnover: €45m

Mercato Metropolitano runs food markets with community and sustainability at its heart. Oh and lots of good food, great beer and tasty cocktails. Established by Andrea Rasca, the first outpost was a pop-up in Milan. In 2016 he found a permanent site in London's Elephant and Castle area and has since added a Mayfair address with plans to launch in Berlin and Milan too.

Rasca, who worked with supermarkets Eataly and Esselunga, has made Mercato a success by ensuring his team and all operators abide by ambitious guidelines and beliefs. There are no single-use plastics; all suppliers are vetted for sustainability; each of the 42 stands has to make a delicious £5 (€5.50) lunch; one stall is always reserved for a refugee who wants to start a food business and another for female entrepreneurs; and hundreds of meals are donated to families who could do with help. In 2019, the market drew in 4 million visitors. It is, says Rasca, proof that "you don't need a big sponsor or government to do good and make money".

Q&A with Andrea Rasca

1. **How is your business different from others in the industry?** We run the company for the benefit of the consumers and local people. Our unique revenue-sharing business model means that all of our traders pay a percentage of their takings as rent rather than a flat rate. We can only be as successful as our vendors are – we experience the difficult times together as well as the good.

2. **How do you build your team?** By attraction. I look for aptitude in people, they need to be positive, curious, trustful, kind, ethical and committed. If they have skills too, even better. They must also have a capacity to drive their own teams and lead them towards their objectives.

36.

Spiritland
London

**The harmonious trio fine-tuning the way
we listen to music, eat and drink**

Founded: 2014
Employees: 50
From idea to reality: 6 months

In 2014 Paul Noble, one of the radio
producers who launched MONOCLE 24,
began hatching a plan with Patrick Clayton-
Malone and Dominic Lake (*all pictured, r-l*)
(the duo behind restaurants Canteen and
Merchants Tavern) to do something about
the disappearance of spaces in which to
appreciate music. "The care and attention
that people put into listening to music have
evaporated," says Noble. "We wanted to
re-engage music but in a hospitable setting."

In 2016 the trio opened Spiritland, a
café, bar and radio studio in King's Cross.
The venue is packed with high-end audio
equipment, a joint effort with UK-based
loudspeaker manufacturer Living Voice, and it
hits just the right note. Following its success,
they launched Spiritland Headphone Bar,
a retail space in Mayfair, and a restaurant
and bar in Royal Festival Hall. Each of the
outposts surpass the regular tropes expected
of a bar, restaurant or shop. Spiritland has
found a way to make people sit down, pipe
down and fall back in love with music.

Q&A with Paul Noble
1. **How did you come up with the idea?**
   Spiritland started with two inspirational trips:
   one to the listening bars of Japan, and the other
   to a high-end hi-fi show in Munich. This sparked
   a chain of thought about how listening to music
   might be reimagined in London.
2. **What advice would you have given yourself
   at the beginning?** Grow quickly and capitalise
   on momentum.
3. **What does company culture mean to you?**
   At the heart of what we do are credibility
   and commitment. We endeavour to stay
   true to our musical mission despite the
   financial challenges.

37.
Zingerman's Deli
Ann Arbor, Michigan

The deli where a sense of place and a dose of anarchy have ensured success

Founded: 1982
Employees: 600
Annual turnover: €50,000

Not many executives would cite anarchism as a major influence on their management style. But then few are quite like Ari Weinzweig, the leather-jacket-wearing co-founder of a food-business empire in the US city of Ann Arbor. When he re-read his anarchist books from his student days, Weinzweig found many of the radical principles were present in his own company, Zingerman's Community of Businesses, which started life with a simple delicatessen in 1982.

"I was the only one weird enough to read all this stuff and all the business stuff at the same time," says Weinzweig. "So I was really shocked at how much anarchism was aligned with 'progressive business'." Refusing to drive nationwide growth with a cookie-cutter formula, he has instead concentrated on opening connected food businesses based in the small city of just 120,000 people and a history of activism. Today, Weinzweig's 12 businesses include a farm, bakery and Korean restaurant.

Q&A with Ari Weinzweig

1. **What advice would you have given yourself at the beginning?** The simple things are important – like knowing all of your employees' names, no matter how large your company gets.
2. **What's the biggest challenge of your sector?** It's a *lot* of work and margins are thin at best. It has not typically been a high-paying industry so it's a hard way for folks at every level to make the same money they make in other industries for doing less work. We're trying to change that, slowly but surely.
3. **What's the best thing about being your own boss?** The way we work – collaboratively and with a lot of consensus and open meetings. I'm not sure I fit into the "boss" category as others do.

38.
Mia Mia
Tokyo

The neighbourhood café dedicated to serving its community

Founded: 2020
Initial capital: €75,000
Became profitable after: 1 year

Situated in Higashi Nagasaki, a residential area unknown to many Tokyoites, Mia Mia defies the traditional rule of opening a café in a location with heavy foot traffic and great access. But its second-to-none hospitality has convinced people that it's worth visiting (repeatedly) from afar. When owners Rie and Vaughan Allison found a vacant old boutique in 2019, they trusted their instincts. "The area used to be home to young artists and still accommodates everyone and anyone. It had potential to generate a new flow of people and become a cultural hub," says Rie.

An architect by trade, Rie was responsible for renovating the space while Vaughan, a coffee enthusiast, put together an impressive array of beans. The café is first and foremost dedicated to serving the community: "We're the only place around here that is open from 08.00," says Vaughan. The duo have a list of future projects, including making public benches and producing a Higashi Nagasaki neighbourhood guide.

Q&A with Rie and Vaughan Allison

1. **How did you come up with the idea?** We knew that we wanted to create a special kind of coffee shop – one that was a gathering place, where staff were genuinely interested in customers, and where people would converse and recognize each other the next time they visited.
2. **What's the biggest challenge of your sector?** Japan's coffee culture is dominated by coffee chains, convenience stores and vending machines. Many Japanese people still consider independent coffee shops to be a special weekend visit.
3. **How do you build your team?** We build our team by being part of the team: we do the fun jobs together and we do the tough jobs together.

39.
Wihayo
Amsterdam

The creatives who took a shot at mixing up the spirits scene

Founded: 2016
Employees: 3 (part-time)
Annual turnover: €70,000

Nathalie Ji Yun Kranenburg and Dylan Griffith (*both pictured, Griffith on left*) spent two years trying to distil the first-ever European batch of soju, South Korea's national spirit. A clear, traditionally rice-based liquor that can be drunk neat or in cocktails, soju is the world's best-selling spirit by volume but remains little known outside Asia. After returning from a trip to meet long-lost family in Seoul, Dutch-Korean Kranenburg wanted to change that.

"The soju you get drunk on there is the cheap stuff," she explains. "What I wanted was to elevate the quality of the product while giving it a Dutch spin." So she joined up with Griffith, creative director and founder of design studio Smörgåsbord, on branding and packaging, and historic distillery Herman Jansen. In 2018, Wihayo was born – a double-distilled soju made from rice and malted barley ground in a centuries-old windmill. It has since sold 7,000 bottles and can be found in five countries around Europe, with global distribution in the pipeline.

Q&A with Nathalie Ji Yun Kranenburg
1. **How long until the business became profitable?** It has taken about four years. Patience, determination and a long-term vision have been imperative. We were naive to think we could run a successful spirits business alongside full-time jobs.
2. **What's the best thing about being your own boss?** Flexibility.
3. **What does company culture mean to you?** We rarely sit in the same room these days but what I love is knowing that everyone in our extended Wihayo family has a shared belief that we've created a unique product and we're 100 per cent committed to spreading the word.

40.
Weeds and More
Singapore / Malaysia

The collective that's rooting for change with a farm fresh alternative

Founded: 2016
Employees: 4
Annual turnover: €750,000

While working as a food journalist, Leisa Tyler unearthed details of the quantity of produce being imported from Europe and Australia to Singapore and Malaysia. "It just seemed ludicrous that we were flying in all these products that weren't even fresh and had these huge carbon miles attached," she says. In 2016, Tyler and her husband Ewout Kemner founded the farming collective Weeds and More. Its aim? To cut the amount of fruit and vegetables that touch down in Singapore and Malaysia by growing European varieties closer to home.

Tyler had no farming experience so she sought help from organic farmers, restaurateurs and chefs. She also spent two years experimenting with seeds to see what suited the soil and climate, as well as convincing farmers it would be worth it. Today Weeds and More partners with four ethically run smallholdings in Malaysia, growing more than 10 tonnes of produce every month and supplying some 60 varieties of European herbs and vegetables.

Q&A with Leisa Tyler

1. **How did you come up with the idea?** I had a bet with a restaurateur friend who claimed it wouldn't be possible to grow French breakfast radishes in Malaysia that were as delicious as those from France. I decided to prove him wrong.
2. **How do you build your team?** We rarely look at résumés – anybody can learn a new skill but few can learn a new attitude.
3. **What does company culture mean to you?** Listening to what all team members have to say, regardless of salary or education.
4. **What's the biggest challenge of your sector?** The perception that if something is imported or foreign, it has a higher value.

41.

Plain Goods
New Preston, Connecticut

The design duo sharing their passion for the simple and well made

Founded: 2015
Employees: 10
Became profitable after: 4 years

Plain Goods, a home, clothing and vintage shop first opened in a small space off New Preston's main drag in 2015. Since then, it has moved to a two-storey building a few metres from its original home. "Who knew that this little business that started in a 700-square-foot cottage would have become what it is?" says Michael DePerno, who co-owns Plain Goods with his partner (in business and life) Andrew Fry (*both pictured, DePerno on left*).

This is the kind of place that people will travel for not just because New Preston is idyllic but also because the shop stocks items that can be hard to find, even in New York; they include French canvas umbrellas, textiles from Lithuania and pottery from South Korea. To source these distinctive items, DePerno and Fry embark on buying trips to Europe, where they pound through markets and meet various designers and vendors. It's unequivocally a labour of love. "We have a lot of return customers, which is great," says DePerno. "We really care about giving people something unique and special."

Q&A with Michael DePerno and Andrew Fry

1. **How did you come up with the idea?** Michael owned and managed shops in New York, Los Angeles and Northern California – curating beautiful things has always been his passion. Andrew's background in corporate fashion made the concept a natural evolution.

2. **What advice would you have given yourself at the beginning?** Consult with a talented and capable systems specialist and the best finance/business advisor.

3. **How did you secure funding?** To date, we are fully self-funded.

4. **What's the best thing about being your own boss?** We can bring our dogs to work!

42.

Graanmarkt 13
Antwerp

The Belgian retailer that doesn't buy into trends

Founded: 2010
Employees: 20
Annual turnover: €3.5m

Graanmarkt 13 has been a paragon of good retail since 2010. At a time when many bricks-and-mortar shops are struggling worldwide, it has maintained a successful brand built on products that are made to last. The shop is housed in a neoclassical townhouse on a leafy square in Belgium's second city. Inside, everything on offer – from shirts to handmade ceramics – has been carefully selected by owners Ilse Cornelissens and Tim Van Geloven.

"We don't sell trends but objects for life. We focus on ageless and durable labels and designers," says Cornelissens. To complement their philosophy, there's a restaurant on the lower ground floor, an upstairs rental apartment and rooftop herb garden that supplies the kitchen with produce and honey. Twice a year, the Belgian-Dutch couple also host a secondhand market where customers can hand in and sell worn clothing – and spend their earnings on new products in the shop.

Q&A with Tim Van Geloven

1. **How did you come up with the idea?** We dreamt of founding a place where food, fashion, beauty, art and more could come together. We'd moved from Amsterdam to Antwerp and found the perfect abandoned building for the project.
2. **How do you build your team?** Believe in their skills, allow them to explore these skills and trust them: a great team gives you the power to grow.
3. **What does company culture mean to you?** Our company culture is very much like a family. We've created a house where each floor tells a different story and where people should feel at home. It is a family business and everyone working here should feel part of that family.

43.
Bunkitsu
Tokyo

The pay-for-entry bookshop that's reigniting a passion for print

Founded: 2018
Employees: 20
From idea to reality: 1 year

Bunkitsu is a game-changing bookshop in Tokyo. Conceived by one of Japan's largest books distributors, Nippon Shuppan Hanbai, it charges an entry fee of ¥1,650 (€12). It may seem elitist but the company believes its approach will have the opposite effect and reawaken an appreciation for books. "Our mission is to create spaces to communicate the value of print publications to as many people as possible," says Kengo Takeda, the project's leader.

Takeda's team curates the extensive books inventory (which covers everything from fashion to food and management to health) and has invested in creating an atmosphere that makes spending time here feel worthwhile. The two-storey space is designed to let people linger and explore the shelves at their own pace. A quiet reading zone and research room are only accessible past the admission-fee barrier but the magazine rack is free to browse. "Thirty to 40 per cent of customers buy something," says Takeda. "We believe in the power of bookshops."

Q&A with Kengo Takeda
1. **How do you build your team?** There should be different ideas and opinions in a team but the key is respecting the vision and work ethic of others. Everyone has strengths and weaknesses, so I try to play to people's strengths.
2. **What's the biggest challenge of your sector?** I think people are feeling less attached to books – perhaps because there are so many other means to acquire information. So the challenge is about how to communicate the value of print publications.
3. **What sets Bunkitsu apart?** We provide a variety of services – for example, we can ship purchases to customers and offer this service for free if they spend more than ¥11,000 (€82).

44.

Prick
London

The sharp plant-seller with a love for her neighbourhood

Founded: 2016
Employees: 2
From idea to reality: 18 months

Gynelle Leon left a career as a fraud and compliance analyst to pursue a fascination with flowers. She had completed a floral design course and a year-long internship at an east-London florist when she realised that an increasing number of people were after indoor plants. As a collector of succulents herself, she found it difficult to find retailers that would help her source new plants.

Having discovered there was not one dedicated cactus and succulent shop in London, she decided to open her own – and call it Prick. "It's kind of a joke but when I told people, they thought it was perfect," she says. Leon found that her time-strapped clientele appreciated low-maintenance plants. That's what made her shop a success, together with a commitment to her neighbourhood of Dalston: Leon organises events at the shop called Cactus and Chill for locals to meet. "People come back time after time – and it's not just for the cacti. We have this 'family' and we all love plants. This is more than a shop: we cultivate relationships."

Q&A with Gynelle Leon

1. **What advice would you have given yourself at the beginning?** I had no business experience, so I went into this like a creative project. I wasn't really thinking about how to set up systems. I would ask myself: how will you make it grow?

2. **What are the benefits of being based in London?** This city loves something new and unusual. If you're willing to come up with something that nobody's ever heard of, people will probably be into it. Also, it's a place with a good sense of humour.

3. **What's the best thing about being your own boss?** To have an idea and run with it. You don't have to okay it with anyone.

45.

Industrie Africa
Dar es Salaam

**The Tanzanian platform bringing
African fashion to the rest of the world**

Founded: 2018
Employees: 4
From idea to reality: 18 months

For Nisha Kanabar, creating a platform
showcasing African fashion was about sharing
a richer narrative about the continent and
making it accessible for shoppers. "It was
important to enable consumers to buy the
products, not just to make a directory," says
Tanzanian-born Kanabar. She launched
Industrie Africa as an information-packed
platform in 2018, then e-commerce in
2020. Today it's not dissimilar to luxury
online retailer Net-a-Porter, offering global
consumers the chance to discover fashion
that might otherwise be hard to find.

For outsiders, and even those within the
continent, sourcing fashion in African cities
that haven't had as much media coverage as
European and US centres can be challenging.
Kanabar, who is based in Tanzania's largest
city Dar Es Salaam, admits that prior to
launching Industrie Africa she had little idea
of what was going on in, say, Nairobi. "If we
found it so difficult as Africans to access these
spaces, how difficult would it be for the rest of
the world to find them?" she says.

Q&A with Nisha Kanabar
1. **What's the biggest challenge of your sector?**
   There's very little precedent or blueprint for
   success in African e-commerce, and every
   roadblock requires you to think outside the box
   to find solutions that are sustainable, using very
   little information.
2. **What are the benefits of being based in
   Tanzania?** Our local industry is strong on
   community – being so plugged into our market
   is a significant part of our culture and identity.
3. **How do you build your team?** With great
   intention. We are natively digital as a company,
   and based across five different countries, so a
   digital mindset as well as ambition is essential.

46.

News & Coffee
Barcelona

The neighbourhood kiosk betting against the narrative

Founded: 2019
Employees: 10
Turnover: €300,000

When Pablo Pardo (*pictured*), Davide Datti and Gautier Robial realised that newsstands in Barcelona were selling more gadgetry and snacks than magazines and newspapers, they knew something had to be done.

Since 2010, 120 of the city's 400 kiosks had closed. So the trio launched News & Coffee: sat on the Passeig Sant Joan in the Eixample neighbourhood, stacked with hard-to-find titles and serving speciality coffee, the stall offers inspiration and human connection. "Nobody had thought about how to give these places a new lease of life," says Pardo. While Pardo used to work for some of Barcelona's top hotels and restaurants, Robial had a more corporate background. The latter's wife, artist Yaël Hupert, took charge of choosing the kiosk's selection of titles. "We had a lot of in-house skills, which allowed us to optimise things," says Robial. They have since opened another Barcelona outpost and started a franchise model – they now have six kiosks (plus a concept shop and mobile unit) to their name.

Q&A with Gautier Robial
1. **How long did it take to get from idea to reality?** It took two and a half years of market study and then six months between financing and opening.
2. **How long until the business became profitable?** Six months. We created the model so it would work at a smaller scale and quickly.
3. **What was your initial capital?** The three partners chipped in €20,000 each and we've since added a bank loan of similar value. We've been exposed to big investment offers, the temptation is there but until you've learned your craft and feel you have control, it doesn't make sense to bring people or capital into your project.

47.

City Grange
Chicago

The green-fingered retailer who's teaching the world to grow

Founded: 2019
Employees: 10 full-time (25 in the summer)
Initial capital: €306,000

"Our belief is that the world would be a better place if there were more gardeners in it," says LaManda Joy, founder of Chicago's City Grange gardening centre, which has outposts in Lincoln Square and Beverly. The seed for City Grange was planted back in 2010 when Joy launched the Peterson Garden Project, a social enterprise that teaches people how to grow food on unused urban land. "I realised that garden centres weren't equipped with the things I needed for my gardeners, such as organic plants and good advice," says Joy.

Today, many of Joy's customers who started as novice gardeners have become regular shoppers, having discovered just how rewarding growing your own can be. As an educator, City Grange offers classes that cover everything from seedling basics to pollinator plants, which instructs people on how to lure butterflies and birds to their windowsills. "The best way to ensure lifelong gardeners is to teach them, so education is the cornerstone of what we do," says Joy.

Q&A with LaManda Joy

1. **What advice would you have given yourself at the beginning?** That running a business is more challenging, and rewarding, than you can imagine. I would also remind myself that nothing big happens alone – you need a team of like-minded believers; they are any company's greatest asset.
2. **What's the best thing about being your own boss?** It's a constant exercise in creativity and self evaluation: if something isn't working, it's on you.
3. **How do you build your team?** Hire slow. Although we're still in the process of building our core team, it is obvious that the people with the greatest longevity are the ones who connect with our mission.

48.

Officine Universelle Buly
Paris

The historic brand that has been brought back to life

Founded: 2014 (originally 1803)
Employees: 500
From idea to reality: 1 year

When it comes to breathing new life into heritage brands, Ramdane Touhami is a seasoned professional. In 2006 (along with his wife Victoire de Taillac) he revived French candlemakers Cire Trudon which was originally established in 1643. The endeavour proved a huge global success. "After Cire Trudon, I wanted to move more into the perfume and cosmetics industry," says Touhami, who sold his stakes in the business in 2010.

The idea for Buly came to him while reading Honoré de Balzac's 1837 book *César Birotteau* which tells the story of a French perfumer who lost his fortune. After discovering that the character was based on a historical figure called Jean-Pierre Bully, Touhami and De Taillac acquired the name and launched Officine Universelle Buly. Today, Buly has shops in nine countries and manufactures more than 900 products including alcohol-free scents and paraben-free cosmetics, all elegantly packaged in old-fashioned vials and glass jars.

Q&A with Ramdane Touhami

1. **What advice would you have given yourself at the beginning?** Read contracts *carefully*. And if you're looking for investors, choose them wisely – think about whether you really need them.
2. **What does company culture mean to you?** Everyone should be learning – me included.
3. **How do you build your team?** When someone leaves my design studio, I let the team decide who they're going to hire as a replacement. I put a lot of energy, however, into finding the right shop staff. You can have the nicest packaging and make the best product but if your client is treated badly in the store everything is undone. They're the face of the brand.

49.
ST Company
Kiryu, Japan

The rural fashion store that's become a destination of its own

Founded: 2018
Employees: 25
From idea to reality: 15 months

"If you serve truly delicious food in the middle of nowhere, people will come. This rule should apply to fashion too," says Toshio Tamaki, the retail veteran behind ST Company. Open since 2018, this venture in Kiryu, Gunma – a town with a population of 110,000 situated a two-hour drive from Tokyo – has set a new standard for destination fashion shops.

Tamaki takes an old-school approach to business, preferring handshakes to emails: "I have to see everything, clothes and people, face-to-face," he says. When he is not out and about, the 72-year-old is serving customers in the shop. This earnest work ethic has won him an invaluable network of designers, customers and colleagues. Today, the shop is constantly attracting new customers with its impressive inventory of labels for men and women. There's a terrace, café and pop-up space to complete the mix. But Tamaki maintains his sharp focus. "Our customers come to us to have a personal experience; shop from 'our' staff and get 'our' styling tips."

Q&A with Toshio Tamaki

1. **How did you secure funding?** I secured a loan from a bank and used savings. In total, I started the business with ¥100m [€751,000].
2. **How do you build your team?** I'm old-fashioned – I treat everyone as part of the family. I can be very strict but I'm honest and equal to everyone and of course I lead by example. I like to observe how new staff grow – some of my employees have worked with me for 30 years.
3. **What advice would you have given yourself at the beginning?** Aim high. The sales will follow. A strong inventory of labels isn't enough, offer style tips too. It's the same as food – people want to know how to cook the ingredients.

50.

Type Books
Toronto

The Canadian bookshop where readers help to set the tone

Founded: 2006
Employees: 13
From idea to reality: 1 year

Joanne Saul and Samara Walbohm (*both pictured, Saul on left*) founded Type Books in 2006. "When we started, Amazon was on the rise and so was Indigo [Canada's largest book retailer]," says Saul. "Neighbourhood bookshops were disappearing." Now Type has three locations across the city and is one of the best-loved names within Toronto's rich constellation of independent sellers.

   "Our bookshops are a collaborative project," says Saul. "We have incredible staff who help us choose the books. But our selection is also influenced by the people who come in and talk to us." Literacy programmes for children, readings and signings, and exhibitions by local artists are also among Type's offerings. A recent innovation is the "mystery bag" of books, which costs CA$100 (€68) and is personally curated by one of Type's booksellers (the novelist Margaret Atwood is among those to have bought one). "In those bags we're able to do what we love, which is to put the right books in people's hands," says Saul.

Q&A with Joanne Saul
1. **What's the biggest challenge of your sector?** Margin and not being able to control the prices – they are generally printed directly onto books. If someone wants to shop online, we can't compete with that, nor do we want to.
2. **How do you build your team?** I think our team builds us. Many of our hires are through contacts from our current staff or even customers.
3. **How did you secure funding?** What we imagined for our business was so against the wisdom at that time that finding capital was impossible. Many thought we were crazy. Thankfully, we had some savings, and our families and friends were willing to take a risk and help us.

51.
Shila
Athens

The newbies putting Greek boutique hotels on the map

Founded: 2018
Employees: 6
From idea to reality: 2 years

Luxurious and design-driven but with a laidback, distinctly Athenian feel, the six-suite Shila Athens is the brainchild of Greek creative director Eftihia Stefanidi (*pictured*) and New York-based entrepreneur Shai Antebi. French interior specialist Anna Bonnet was the project's head designer. Following two years of hard work, they had planned to open in April 2020. Then the pandemic hit, forcing them to delay until June and contend with a drop in tourist numbers. "We knew it would be challenging," says Stefanidi with a wry smile. "But none of us are from a traditional business background – we're all makers – so we knew we could make it work."

And they have. On top of asking fellow entrepreneurs and creatives to stay in the hotel while they fine-tuned their service, they've hosted photoshoots, launched a line of furniture and design objects, and started a membership club to attract locals. "The aim is to let people feel something unique when they come to Athens," explains Stefanidi.

Q&A with Eftihia Stefanidi

1. **What advice would you have given yourself at the beginning?** Follow your vision and don't let the noise disturb you. Dare to go against the norm even if everyone else believes you are crazy.
2. **What are the benefits of being based in Athens?** Timing and culture. The city is undergoing a gradual expansion in the hospitality and cultural sector and Athens has an anarchic feel that inspires you to push the boundaries.
3. **How do you build your team?** We prioritise working with passionate individuals who love what they do and make our project their own.
4. **What's the biggest challenge in hospitality?** Keeping everyone happy.

52.

Souk el-Tayeb & Tawlet
Beirut

The Lebanese hospitality maverick with a social mission

Founded: 2004
Employees: 120
Became profitable after: 5 years

Socially-minded entrepreneur Kamal Mouzawak has always been a trailblazer. He set up Lebanon's first farmer's market, Souk el Tayeb, in 2004 and followed it in 2009 with Tawlet, a laidback restaurant where women from around the country cook delicious regional dishes. He also opened a chain of boutique hotels around the country.

Then came the devastating Beirut port blast in August 2020, which killed more than 200 and destroyed half the city, including the company's headquarters. At first, Mouzawak thought it was game over. But through sheer determination, he and his team have rebuilt. There's a new indoor market space, a 55-cover restaurant with a small food shop, new offices, and a new community kitchen, Matbakh el Kell, which serves free meals daily to those in need. He's even expanding abroad into Paris. "It took a lot of strength, effort and faith to build so fast in the middle of the ruins," says Mouzawak. "We just had to do it, to build, to go on and to create life to erase all the death."

Q&A with Kamal Mouzawak

1. **How long did it take to get from initial idea to reality?** Did we get there? I'm not sure we ever will – it's a journey – but getting from a personal initiative to the start of an institution took five years, when in 2009 Christine Codsi joined as a business partner.
2. **How do you build your team?** By putting my trust in people.
3. **What does company culture mean to you?** A company, a family or any relationship is built on complementarity.
4. **What are the benefits of being based in Beirut?** For me, it wasn't a choice – I was there and I had to make a change.

53.

Schloss Schauenstein
Fürstenau, Switzerland

The lauded chef proving you can reach your peak in a remote location

Founded: 2003
Employees: 70
From idea to reality: 1 year

Life moves slowly in the village of Fürstenau – at least until you enter the kitchens of chef Andreas Caminada. He opened his first restaurant Schloss Schauenstein in the Swiss Canton of Graubünden in 2003, just 20 minutes from where he grew up. "I always wanted to run my own restaurant," says Caminada, who discovered his love for cooking at the age of 14. He went on to become one of the world's youngest chefs to be awarded three Michelin stars.

When it came to starting his own venture, it wasn't a city that Caminada chose: "I knew I'd want to open a restaurant close to home because I was familiar with the region and its produce," he says. Nonetheless he had reservations. "I wondered whether this valley would be a fitting destination but we went for it," he says. Today, guests travel many miles to dine at Schloss Schauenstein and he has since launched a hotel-cum-bakery and vegetarian outpost. He has also formed strong relationships with local suppliers with the aim of bringing life back to Fürstenau.

Q&A with Andreas Caminada
1. **What are the benefits of being based in Fürstenau?** It is magical and full of joy. We are in the middle of Graubünden's exceptional nature and are lucky to be surrounded by some of the most passionate farmers and craftsmen of their kind.
2. **What advice would you have given yourself at the beginning?** Believe in your dreams and stay true to yourself but also be realistic – you have to work hard in order to be a success.
3. **How do you build your team?** We find and foster talented individuals, shape their skills and encourage them to take on more responsibility.

54.
Sleeep
Hong Kong

The sharp-eyed pair who turned sleepless nights into successful slumber

Founded: 2016
Employees: 7 (full-time) 10 (seasonal)
Became profitable after: 18 months

Founded by business-design duo Alex Kot and Jun Rivers (*both pictured, Rivers on left*), Sleeep is a chain of capsule hotels in Hong Kong that specialises in offering shut-eye throughout the day. Guests can book sleep pods for several minutes (or several months) making the business popular with both hardworking locals and visiting tourists. The pair say that those working in banking and the public sector are among Sleeep's most frequent clients. "Some people are just looking for some 'me time'," says Kot.

Kot and Rivers entered a prototype of Sleeep in the Harvard Dean Challenge in 2014; the competition called for designs to alleviate problems tied to urban overpopulation. Sleep deprivation has been an issue for both founders: Kot was diagnosed with sleep apnea as a teenager and Rivers experienced the lasting effects of staying awake for too long while at architecture school. "You can't just fill a gap: you have to go through it and experience it for yourself," says Rivers.

Q&A with Alex Kot
1. **What was your initial capital?** Around HK$1.8m [€168,000] was used to launch the prototype business.
2. **What are the benefits of being based in Hong Kong?** It is one of the most vibrant cities in Asia with the highest real estate cost; people here are desperately looking for a solution to living well. There are also lots of hardworking people who are searching for a more meaningful lifestyle.
3. **How do you build your team?** We attracted a circle of experts who were dissatisfied with the status quo. For example, we hired a professional who is helping us transform our business while we help transform his health and wellbeing.

55.
Trevarefabrikken
Henningsvaer, Norway

The group of friends bringing city life to the Arctic north

Founded: 2014
Employees: 10 full-time (60 in the summer)
From idea to reality: 2 years

The village of Henningsvaer in the Lofoten archipelago of Arctic Norway is home to over 50 companies, many of which are led by young entrepreneurs. Among these, the cultural-centre-cum-hotel Trevarefabrikken is the area's biggest success story. It was founded by Bergen-born brothers Andreas and Martin Hjelle, and two friends, who discovered an abandoned 1940s factory and secured the three-storey space for €200,000.

"We wanted to live a different life in Henningsvaer, where many young creatives like us are moving," says Martin. With 60 people on its books in peak season, it is the town's main employer and welcomes about 20,000 guests every year. Downstairs, the ground floor comprises a restaurant, bar and café while an outdoor area leads to a timber-and-glass panoramic sauna and bar. The friends secured a government grant to expand which led to an upgrade that added six double rooms and a suite, with interiors designed by London studio Jonathan Tuckey.

Q&A with Andreas Hjelle

1. **How did you come up with the idea?** We didn't have an idea to start with. After seeing this unused space and its potential, surrounded by the most beautiful nature, we started creating the space bit by bit. Our growth has been very organic.

2. **What are the benefits of setting up a rural business?** It's definitely more affordable. We would have never had the means to build all of this anywhere close to a city. It allows us to have so much creative freedom.

3. **What does company culture mean to you?** Everything we've done has revolved around an adventurous group of people ready to leave the city behind and relocate to the Arctic.

56.
Stayfolio
Seoul

The side-hustle that grew into a serious revenue generator

Founded: 2015
Employees: 40
Annual turnover: €15m

Stayfolio is a property-rental platform with a difference. The lettings website – a discerning apartment-rental service for design fans – was launched in 2015 by the founders of the Seoul-based architecture firm Z-Lab: Park Jung-hyun, Noh Kyung-rok and Lee Sang-muk (*pictured, from left*). It features the studio's growing portfolio of rental projects, spanning *hanoks* in Seoul to a farmhouse and caravan park on the southern island of Jeju.

The architects redesign and renovate the properties, which are often second or unused homes, and then take charge of the marketing, management and even mood – each address has its own fragrance and music playlist. In return they take a share of the profits. "Our guests have money to spend but they don't just like luxury, they want originality and design too," says Noh. What began as a side hustle has now become a core part of the company. In fact, Stayfolio has proved an effective billboard for the team's architectural talents, attracting new commissions for Z-Lab and fresh capital.

Q&A with Lee Sang-muk

1. **What's the biggest challenge of your sector?** Finding new spaces. Many places look amazing in photos but are not great in reality. We are constantly challenging ourselves.
2. **What does company culture mean to you?** We believe in positive thinking and rather than relying on individual performance, we value the power of teamwork: we may go faster if we go alone, but we can go farther if we do it together. We also value the process rather than the result.
3. **What are the benefits of being based in Seoul?** It is a megacity with 10 million citizens. It is both traditional and modern and has magnificent potential.

57.

Brücke 49
Vals, Switzerland

**The hoteliers who swapped their
nine-to-fives for a better quality of life**

Founded: 2011
Employees: 5
Became profitable after: 1 year

Whenever Thomas Schacht and his wife
Ruth Kramer travelled, they always ended up
dreaming. Having spent 20 years building up
an advertising agency, Danish-born Schacht
had fallen out of love with the business. So he
and Kramer (a designer by trade) acquired
a house in the Swiss town of Vals, renovating
and launching it as guesthouse Brücke 49.

In 2021, Schacht sadly passed away though
Ruth is continuing as the pair intended.
Today, the small outpost is a reference for
rural hospitality from the design of the interior
(heavily Scandinavian in feel) to the pastries
at breakfast. "I used to work from eight until
five," says Kramer. "Now I have time to go
for a walk in the mornings or an ice-cold
dip in the river. It makes you feel alive."
It's this way of life that Brücke 49 instils in
its guests: home-cooked breakfasts are made
from produce delivered to the doorstep while
yoga can be enjoyed at sunrise. It's a haven
where guests go to recharge. "To create your
own vision of how life should be is a daily
inspiration for me," says Kramer.

Q&A with Ruth Kramer
1. **How long did it take to get from initial idea
   to reality?** Two minutes. When we saw the house
   we realised it was too big for just two people and
   a dog. But the building work took eight months.
2. **What advice would you have given to
   yourself at the beginning?** Do it with a plan
   that you feel is 100 per cent your own. You will
   work hard every day but you get to decide how
   your business should be. In the end it is all about
   creating a happy and full life.
3. **What does company culture mean to you?**
   Being one family – we share all our ideas and
   listen to everyone's feedback. We really think
   about and take care of each other.

58.
Rendez-vous
Toulouse

The fashion insiders showing you can start afresh and succeed in a small city

Founded: 2015
Employees: 8
Annual turnover: €1 to €2m

The story of Rendez-vous, one of Europe's best fashion shops, is an encouraging tale of two fashion insiders who'd had enough of the industry and decided to do their own thing. Marc Llorens, who'd worked as a designer in Paris for 15 years, gave it all up and moved to Toulouse where he met Olivier Salette (*both pictured, Llorens on left*), who'd previously worked in merchandising. "We decided to open this small menswear shop with a selection of brands that concentrate on high-quality manufacturing," says Llorens. "We found an old gallery space and relied on a tiny business plan so we could stay small."

Using savings, the pair bought brands they liked to wear and launched RDV, an in-house shirt line. They've mostly focused on "niche brands who have limited distributions on the internet," says Llorens. Since opening the original store they have added an online shop where they put together ensembles with a playful flair, and opened a womenswear outpost two doors up, all while remaining hands-on in all aspects of the business.

Q&A with Marc Llorens
1. **How long did it take to get from initial idea to reality?** We spent six months thinking about the project and drafting the business plan. We started with the first men's shop with a limited selection and launched the online shop soon afterwards.
2. **What's the biggest challenge of your sector?** Fashion is one of the most polluting industries. We are very committed to the environment and want to sell more ethical fashion, with less waste – we are looking for more eco-friendly solutions.
3. **What are the benefits of being based in Toulouse?** The quality of life – it's so much calmer here. We realised that you don't have to be in a capital city to have a successful business.

59.

Jacqueline Rabun
Los Angeles / London

The self-funded jewellery designer crafting wearable works of art

Founded: 1990
Employees: 1
Became profitable after: 3 years

Jacqueline Rabun established her eponymous jewellery-design practice as a personal project. She wasn't a wearer of accessories at the time – until she stumbled across an independent jewellery gallery in Los Angeles, where she discovered the organic, rounded forms that would later define her approach to the craft. "It was like stepping into a gallery of miniature sculptures," she says. "I just fell in love with it."

She promptly secured a job as gallery assistant, which allowed her to experiment with her own designs and perfect her carving techniques. On moving to London in 1990, Rabun launched her inaugural collection of hand-sculpted rings, pendants, bracelets and earrings. That collection, which was self-funded and took nine months to create, won her instant acclaim and attracted clients including Barneys New York and 10 Corso Como. Today, while dividing her time between Los Angeles and the UK, Rabun is still forming the artful pared-back pieces for which she has become globally known.

Q&A with Jacqueline Rabun
1. **What advice would you have given yourself at the beginning?** Take your time and focus on perfecting your design language.
2. **What's the best thing about being your own boss?** The freedom that it gives me to choose how I wish to live my life.
3. **How do you build your team?** My small team is made up of expert craftspeople who are passionate about producing well-made and sustainable pieces. They are all external: this allows me more time to focus on creating.
4. **What are the benefits of being based in both London and Los Angeles?** They are two very different cities with strong creative energies.

60.

Racing Atelier
Oberammergau, Germany

The craftsman whose rural backdrop provides more than just inspiration

Founded: 2014
Employees: 1
Became profitable after: 6 years

"A gut feeling brought me back here," says Leander Angerer of his return to the Bavarian alpine town where he grew up, before studying design at Dessau in Germany and London's Central Saint Martins. "I found this unused carpenter's workshop and started something I couldn't afford to do in the city."

From the workshop that adjoins his home, he creates backpacks from durable leather and sells them to an international clientele. He has one wholesale client; everything else is made-to-order based on direct correspondence with customers, meaning he can manage his workload and supply chain – and minimise waste. In fact, Racing Atelier checks many boxes around responsible manufacturing; the leather, for example, comes from only 25km away. "Being detached from city life and separated from other designers has become a luxury," he says. "It has helped me define my own style. If I want to make a living, I have to communicate the value of manufacturing the product here."

Q&A with Leander Angerer

1. **What advice would you have given yourself at the beginning?** There's only so much you can do yourself: when starting something the way I did, it often seems the only option is to do it all on your own – design, development, production, finances and marketing. It's good to ask for help.

2. **What are the benefits of being based somewhere so remote?** Being detached from the hustle of city life means fewer distractions and a cheaper, calmer life. Plus, it makes for a beautiful backdrop to the workshop.

3. **What's the biggest challenge of your sector?** Successfully communicating the fact that my goods cost as much as they do due to the labour.

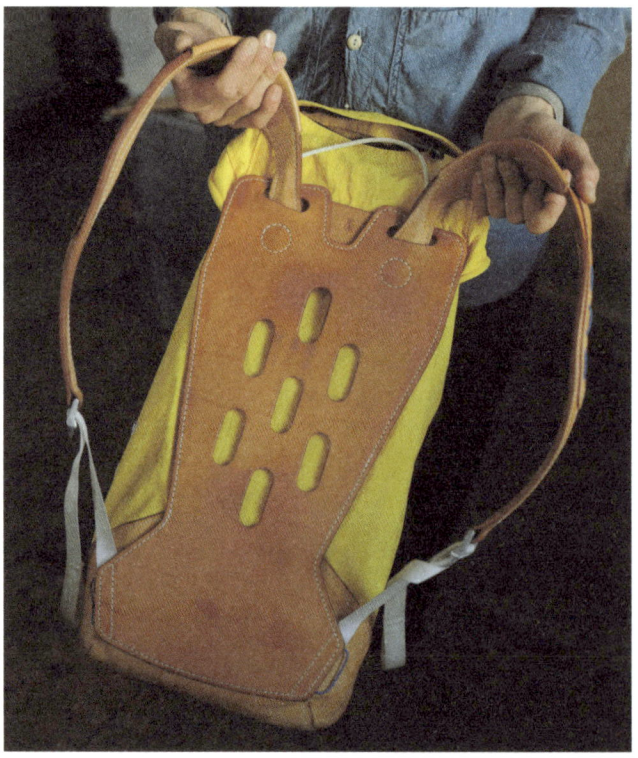

61.

Work Wear Suit
Tokyo

The plumber-turned-entrepreneur who tapped into a new industry

Founded: 2017
Employees: 37 (at parent company OSW)
From idea to reality: 2 years

To say that Yuzo Sekiya's career has followed an unorthodox trajectory is an understatement. Sekiya started out as a plumber working for his father's company before launching his own plumbing business in Tokyo in 2006. But when struggling to recruit young talent in 2016, he had an idea. "We thought we might attract them if our uniform was more stylish," he says. Sekiya's team scoured the globe for a fabric that was durable, comfortable and looked good. "We couldn't find any, so we developed our own."

It was a hit: the uniform they'd created not only attracted young employees, it opened up a new market. Today Work Wear Suit (WWS) – which is owned by Sekiya's company Oasys Style Wear (OSW) – has 1,000 clients in the plumbing, taxi, gardening and hospitality industries, while fashion-conscious consumers snap up the simple jackets, trousers and coats too. It's a smart model for a clothing business because, as Sekiya says, "We have one material for basic, all-season staples. We don't end up with unsold seasonal collections."

Q&A with Yuzo Sekiya

1. **What's the biggest challenge of your sector?** Distinguishing our brand from competitors such as Uniqlo. Although the directions of our products are different, we're often compared. Today, other major workwear makers and suit companies have followed but WWS is a specialised brand so we'll keep sticking to our guns.
2. **What advice would you have given yourself at the beginning?** Look forward to the fun times ahead of you; creating a new business from scratch is not easy and there will be tough moments.
3. **How do you build your team?** I don't like to be alone so at work I want be around many people with positive attitudes.

62.

Ecoalf
Madrid

The environmentalist who's proving it's possible be sustainable and stylish

Founded: 2012
Employees: 130
Annual turnover: €24m

Ecoalf was founded in 2012 and has now developed more than 250 fabrics, crafting trainers from algae and trousers from recycled plastic bottles. This environmental ethos permeates every aspect of the label, from production to shipping. "I convinced textile makers to create recycled fabrics for me," says Ecoalf founder and director Javier Goyeneche. "I made them realise that producing fabrics from ocean waste would give them a business advantage as they would be ahead of the curve."

Too often "sustainability" is thrown around as a marketing ploy. "It's not enough to make something in organic cotton if you are still producing masses that end up in landfill," says Goyeneche. Ecoalf makes its products where the waste is sourced to reduce emissions: it has an Asian warehouse to send orders direct to customers in that continent. Goyeneche started the Ecoalf Foundation in 2015, a non-profit that oversees Upcycling the Oceans, an initiative that removes debris from the ocean's floor.

Q&A with Javier Goyeneche

1. **How long until the business became profitable?** Seven years. Most of the decisions we made at the start weren't profitable in the short-term – we've always been focused on the long-term. Whenever we have taken a decision that we thought was good for the planet it has ended up being good for Ecoalf in the medium-term too.
2. **What's the biggest challenge of your sector?** The business model itself. The fashion industry is the second most-polluting industry in the world and we need to reformulate the idea of buying and tossing, as well as continuous discounts.
3. **What advice would you have given yourself at the beginning?** Always stay true to your values.

63.

Totême
Stockholm

The Scandinavian fashion house with practicality at its core

Founded: 2014
Employees: 66
Annual turnover: €35m

The husband-and-wife team of Karl Lindman and Elin Kling are striving to build a "luxury Scandinavian fashion house on a global arena." After launching their first collection in 2014 (while both were holding down full-time jobs in publishing), they're well on their way to making this a reality. The womenswear brand is beloved for its elegantly understated designs rooted in practicality. "Traditionally a brand might start a collection by creating a mood board," says Kling. "Our design process is different: we start with a purpose. We might think, 'it's Tuesday, I need to get to work and it is raining outside.' So a rain poncho is added to the autumn collection. I like to be nerdy with situation analysis."

It's working: the brand has more than 60 employees, 85 per cent of them women, and in 2020 it unveiled its second Stockholm shop. There are plans to open flagships (or "brand embassies," as Lindman calls them) overseas so that more shoppers can step into Totême's world of cable-knit cashmere sweaters and boxy V-neck blouses.

Q&A with Karl Lindman and Elin Kling

1. **How did you secure funding?** We invested all our savings into the business and looked for a bank that would lend us the rest of the funds needed (which was about half of the initial capital). All the banks we approached turned us down – except one.
2. **What advice would you have given yourself at the beginning?** Be prepared to make tough decisions along the way. Perhaps most importantly, follow your gut feeling and enjoy the process.
3. **What's the best thing about being your own boss?** We are humbled by the fact that we get to work with so many talented individuals. What started as a crazy – and perhaps naive – dream is now a reality shaped and shared by so many.

64.

Eleven Eleven
New Delhi

The clothing label that's weaving an alternative to fast fashion

Founded: 2008
Employees: 360 (including artisans)
Annual turnover: €567,000

This unisex brand, by Shani Himanshu and Mia Morikawa (*pictured*), is a celebration of Indian craftsmanship. Morikawa and Himanshu work with weavers and natural-dyers across the country to create textiles that are used to make garments in New Delhi. They favour traditional techniques such as *chindi* patchwork and *bandhani* tie-dye.

Most of the brand's customers are women in India (where it has 30 stockists) yet it's building an international following thanks to accounts with Matches and Mr Porter. "Our work is a form of resistance: it's anti-industrial and reflects the art of slow living. We found an alternative to fast fashion in the humble handloom fabric," says Morikawa. Yet she also emphasises that this is not your typical business model. "It won't be easy for us to become hugely profitable – that has never been the main driver behind our efforts," she says. "The aim is to generate security for ourselves, our team and contribute to building power in indigenous communities."

Q&A with Eleven Eleven co-founders

1. **What are the benefits of being based in India?**
   India has a lot of traditional craft techniques that have been practiced for many years. To be able to have access to these is a big asset for the brand. The culture here is also rich, deep, diverse and endlessly inspiring.
2. **What's the biggest challenge of your sector?**
   Lead time. We develop our own textiles and some of our development begins a year in advance.
3. **What does company culture mean to you?**
   There is nothing more beautiful than a group of people being able to overcome personal differences, commit to a common goal, cooperate and deliver.

65.

Rejina Pyo
London / Seoul

**The designer who followed her instincts
– and saved her business**

Founded: 2013
Employees: 14 (London) 5 (Seoul)
Became profitable after: 3 years

In 2016, Rejina Pyo (*pictured, on right*) was
on the brink of closing her fashion label. The
South Korean-born, London-based designer's
clothes were not shifting. She decided to
design one last do-or-die collection. "I hadn't
been doing 100 per cent what I wanted to do,"
says Pyo. "I thought I would make this final-
chance collection and if it didn't work out, it
would be because I'm not talented enough."

But it did work out. Pyo followed her
instincts and designed a collection that she
wanted to wear: oversized trench coats in
windowpane check, below-the-knee skirts in
pleated fabric, and a marigold midi-length
dress. Treading the line between fashion and
function, her clothes are flattering and easy
to wear. The label has expanded rapidly: its
offerings now include shoes, bags, jewellery, a
unisex line and, most recently, childrenswear.
For Pyo, the customer is considered at every
step. "I always think, 'What is her salary, can
she afford to spend that?' As a designer, you
need to know who your clothes are sold to.
It has to make sense in the real world."

Q&A with Rejina Pyo

1. **What was your initial capital?** In 2012 I was
   awarded the Han Nefkens Fashion Award, which
   included a commission to create work for the
   Museum Boijmans Van Beuningen in Rotterdam
   as well as a prize fund of €25,000. The prize
   money served as the impetus to start my brand.
2. **What advice would you give yourself at the
   beginning?** Trust your instincts. At the start I was
   listening to advice from so many different people,
   and in many cases doing what they suggested
   even when my gut was telling me otherwise.
3. **How do you build your team?** Slowly. My
   first intern is now our wholesale sales manager
   and worked her way up over seven years.

66.

Tibi
New York

The business-minded creative who used previous experience to succeed

Founded: 1997
Employees: 39
From idea to reality: 3 months

When Amy Smilovic started Tibi she was coming from a business, rather than a design, perspective. A former advertising associate who later worked for American Express, she started the self-funded label in 1997 on her second day living in Hong Kong. Her experience and left-brain mentality were major assets. "I had so much exposure to different income levels and what people would spend," she says. "I can't work out how you would start a label with only a design degree. You need business, you need marketing – you need life experience."

The brand, now headquartered in Manhattan, provides women with modern wardrobe staples: versatile clothes that can be worn "three seasons a year, five different ways," says Smilovic. They are practical pieces with subtle design-focused nuances. Smilovic sees the "need – or at least the perceived need – for newness" as the biggest challenge facing the fashion industry. "Creatively, you are literally turning your ideas upside down a few times a year."

Q&A with Amy Smilovic

1. **How long until the business became profitable?** Six months. I never bit off more than I could chew.
2. **How did you secure funding?** I got my first line of credit based on my turnover. I created a small run, I sold it then reinvested the profit. Over and over. And then I found myself at the point where orders coming in could not be covered by my prior receivables. At that point I applied for a line of credit.
3. **What advice would you have given yourself at the beginning?** In the early years once the business took off, I wish that I'd stayed true to my point of view in terms of what I wanted to design.

67.

Métier London
London

The high-end label cultivating a slower pace and a product that lasts a lifetime

Founded: 2017
Employees: 10
From idea to reality: 3 years

"We're luxury problem solvers," says Melissa Morris, founder of London leather-goods label Métier. She's holding a zip-around backpack in black leather, with clip-off straps that transform it into a tote-style briefcase; inside, there's a removable pouch with pockets for phones, glasses and passports, and sleeves to store a water bottle. "We created this for guys that take the red-eye and go straight from the airport to the office. It's a portable filing cabinet."

Morris started Métier in 2017 after seeing a gap in the market for luxury goods made at a slower-pace. Her bags – all handcrafted in Italy and weather-tested to withstand 20 years of use – are designed to fill a specific day-to-night travel need. "It's about making lives easier and saving our clients' time." Meanwhile, her London shop is a place to slow down; in the small, timber-lined space, which mimics a mid-century ship, a bar serves coffee, cocktails and wine. "You have to be clever with limited space," she says. "Every detail really counts."

Q&A with Melissa Morris

1. **How did you come up with the idea?** After years of travelling, I found that the leather goods that were meant to carry our most cherished belongings weren't optimised for the way we live in the 21st century.

2. **What's the biggest challenge of your sector?** Many clients are used to a faster pace in luxury design. We do the opposite. We create a limited amount of perfected products to last for life. We focus on building trust and relationships with our clients rather than encouraging them to replace what they already have.

3. **How do you build your team?** Slowly and carefully. There are no egos.

68.

This is Us
Lagos

The creative duo championing the community alongside their own brand

Founded: 2016
Employees: 12
From idea to reality: 4 years

Based in Lagos, This Is Us clothing brand's indigo-dyed uniform-wear isn't just "100 per cent Nigerian end-to-end", as husband-and-wife owners Oroma Cookey-Gam and Osione Itegboje say. The company started when the pair undertook a cross-country trip in search of local materials. They ended up at the cotton farms of Funtua in Katsina State. Today, its cotton is grown, woven, dyed and sewn into clothing here. "We realised how much exists in our textiles industry that's under the radar," says Cookey-Gam.

This Is Us also connects young makers with farmers and manufacturers. One business that has benefitted is the Kofar Mata dye pits: there was only one operating pit when the brand discovered it. This Is Us began dyeing its clothes there in a process unchanged in 500 years and now the facility is undergoing a resurgence. "We want to be in the middle of the talent, the resources, the craftsmanship. We want to create something useful for the industry."

Q&A with This Is Us co-founders

1. **How did you come up with the idea?** We were trying to find locally made cotton and it was impossible. So we started researching and discovered an entire developed and underutilised cotton industry that was almost completely untapped. We decided that we wanted to design and showcase Nigerian resources and culture.

2. **What advice would you have given yourself at the beginning?** We'd do it exactly the same way – but would just be more appreciative of the time it takes to do things properly here.

3. **What's the best thing about being your own boss?** Being able to plan our time and our work around our family.

69.

Country of Origin
London / Wigston, UK

The independent knitwear brand that chose not to follow the flock

Founded: 2013
Employees: 8
From idea to reality: 2 years

It hasn't all been smooth sailing for Ben Taylor and Alice Liptrot, the founders of knitwear label Country of Origin. "We initially had a small workshop in south London under a railway arch but struggled to keep up with capacity," says Taylor. At one point, they were producing 5,000 sweaters in the space every season. "We had only two knitting machines and a couple of staff, and the orders from Japan increased year on year. It was chaos," says Taylor.

Several years on, though, and the brand has a much more solid production line: it owns a factory in Wigston, Leicestershire, historically a knitwear manufacturing town. "There's a huge demand for UK-made knitwear worldwide; it's the gold standard," says Taylor. They opened the factory – an unusual step for an independent brand – in partnership with industry veteran Saïd Saleh. It enables them to experiment freely. "We can go to the factory as much as we want and try new things out with more complicated designs," says Liptrot.

Q&A with Ben Taylor

1. **What advice would you have given yourself at the beginning?** We pretty much started the company fresh out of university. In retrospect it would have probably been wise to get some industry experience before diving in!

2. **What are the benefits of being based in the UK?** It is home to a wealth of talented people. Since Brexit, life has become more difficult from a business and cultural perspective but, despite everything, London remains an incredibly vibrant city.

3. **What's the biggest challenge of your sector?** Staffing – we struggle to find skilled technicians or people willing to be trained up.

70.

Atelier Saman Amel
Stockholm

The pair measuring up fashion's future and offering a new take on tailoring

Founded: 2015
Employees: 5
Initial capital: €2,000

Saman Amel and Dag Granath (*both pictured, Amel on left*), the pair behind the Stockholm atelier, bring a refreshing edge to tailoring. Since 2012 the childhood friends have created made-to-measure tuxedos, suits and blazers but also overcoats, knitwear and jeans. "Made to measure doesn't have to be formal," says Granath. "Having things custom-made is something that people will be doing more in the future. Retailers are either going to have to be humongous, like Amazon, or small actors who will need to be very niche and will basically be in the business of loyalty."

And what better way to cultivate loyalty than by creating a perfectly fitted item for each client – and enjoying a drink and a chat in the process? In late 2020 the pair opened a store-cum-atelier in central Stockholm to do just that. Although difficult to scale, made-to-order businesses drastically reduce waste and are an efficient, low-risk model. "Our ambition has never been to have 100,000 clients but 1,000 really good clients who we work with for a longer time," says Granath.

Q&A with Dag Granath
1. **How long until the business became profitable?** With no capital to start with and without taking on investors we were forced to be profitable from day one. Growing organically and building an enjoyable life has always been the goal.
2. **What does company culture mean to you?** Saman's father once told us to "always take care of each other". I think investing in your relationships is the most important thing for wellbeing of both your staff and your business.
3. **What's the biggest challenge of your sector?** Fewer social situations require formal dress so tailoring is increasingly becoming a lifestyle choice – you can have more fun and be creative with it.

71.

The Modern House
London

The estate agency curating a tempting new look

Founded: 2005
Employees: 60
Turnover: €7m

The Modern House might be in the business of selling properties but that's where its affinity with estate agencies ends. Founded in London by Matt Gibberd (*pictured*) and Albert Hill, it features homes that embody modern living – be they design classics conceived by great architects or period homes that have been adapted for today's lifestyle.

Both Gibberd and Hill started out as journalists and it was only after discovering a curated platform for selling property in America – as well as receiving a small, unexpected inheritance – that the pair decided to launch their own business. "To approach home sale listings from an editorial approach, as opposed to a transactional viewpoint, was something that came naturally to us. We knew it would set us apart," says Hill. The Modern House has since grown to include its own editorial output: there's an online journal, podcast and a biannual magazine. "I started my career knowing that I had to work with a print magazine because there's nothing quite like it," says Gibberd.

Q&A with Albert Hill

1. **What advice would you have given yourself at the beginning?** Be bolder. When you see something is working you should double down on it. Have the courage of your convictions – when you are doing something that no one else is doing and feel nervous about being out on a limb that's when you're doing something right.
2. **What's the biggest challenge of your sector?** The stakes are high both financially and emotionally when it comes to selling houses, so getting the right staff is crucial.
3. **How did you build your team?** We have purposefully recruited from outside the property sector, largely hiring people with an arts background.

72.

Barkyn
Matosinhos, Portugal

The dog lovers creating Southern Europe's top pet wellness brand

Founded: 2017
Employees: 55
From idea to reality: 3 months

The pet-care industry has grown to become a lucrative market, valued at around €77bn worldwide – and one of the most exciting start-ups in this space is Barkyn. Founded in 2017 by the Portuguese duo André Jordão and Ricardo Macedo (*both pictured, Macedo on left*), it is a highly personalised subscription service for dog owners. Customers receive a monthly box of nutritious dog food, with health perks such as dedicated access to a remote online vet, a free annual health check and Barkyn Complex, the brand's own supplement.

"It's a very emotional market," says Jordão. "Your dog is like a member of your family so we wanted to build a service that was tailored to the individual needs of each dog." Currently operating in Portugal, Spain and Italy, Barkyn has been steadily growing since its inception, having raised a further €3m from a food tech investor in 2021. It's proof that a human approach paired up with quality products is always a good bet – even for our four-legged friends.

Q&A with André Jordão
1. **How did you come up with the idea?** I own two dogs and I wanted to solve some issues involved in taking care of them. They hated going to the vet, I was always forgetting to place an order for more pet food and I didn't have any advice for the right food and care. So we created a service that simplifies all that in one single point of contact.
2. **What's the biggest challenge of your sector?** Fierce competition from large e-commerce websites – they don't deliver a service like we do but are aggressive and have a large customer base.
3. **What advice would you have given yourself at the beginning?** Spend more time testing storytelling and your core offering.

73.

The Cultivist
London / New York

The innovative art experts monetising their inside knowledge

Founded: 2015
Employees: 19
Turnover: €2.5m

Marlies Verhoeven and Daisy Peat (*both pictured, Verhoeven on left*) had been working on auction house Sotheby's VIP programme when they realised there was a wider public who wanted to enjoy similar privileges to top-level collectors. The Cultivist is a membership-only club (with capped numbers to ensure appropriate service) devoted to meeting an art lover's every need: given it's not a loyalty programme aimed at encouraging sales, the team can recommend whatever they feel is best. "I think that makes the relationship more authentic and real," says Verhoeven.

For an annual fee of $2,500 (€2,200 in Europe), members get fast-track entry to more than 150 museums and institutions, access to countless trade fairs, private tours of exhibitions and visits to artist studios in cities around the globe. Today, there are offices in London, New York, Shanghai, Los Angeles and Brussels – as well as a network of 40 collaborators on the ground. Activities have also expanded and a lower-level membership (priced at $40 or €34 a month) is on offer.

Q&A with Marlies Verhoeven
1. **What advice would you have given yourself at the beginning?** The sales are what's going to keep you going, developing and innovating. If you focus too much on everything else, you'll lose sight of the revenue that's going to fund the rest of the business.
2. **What's the best thing about being your own boss?** Running with ideas that you know intuitively are right.
3. **What does company culture mean to you?** It means people come to work happy and, therefore, are more productive – and I think it is driven by the top and how management behave. We're not the type to come up with some slogan. In the team, everyone just has to be nice.

74.

Dabbavelo
Zürich

The food delivery service that is fair and environmentally aware

Founded: 2019
Employees: 8 (plus 50 drivers)
Initial capital: €91,000

"We were angry at the rubbish," says Basil Engler, co-founder of Zürich food delivery company Dabbavelo, established in 2019. The idea is inspired by the circular system perfected by Mumbai's *dabbawalas*, a metal-lunchbox delivery and return service. In Dabbavelo's case, peckish users choose a restaurant on its platform and pay a deposit for a plastic food container. Customers then return the vessel the next time they order food, or they can drop it off at Dabbavelo's offices. "It's important to use something more than once," says Engler. "Our containers are used maybe 150 or 200 times."

Dabbavelo hasn't stopped there. Its food is delivered only by bicycle and Engler, who has been a courier himself, knows that this "tough job" should be remunerated appropriately. Its delivery workers receive CHF25 (€23) an hour and there are plans to expand the current network of riders. While challenges remain, profits are pumped into tweaking the packaging and ensuring more restaurants are taking part in the scheme.

Q&A with Basil Engler

1. **What's the biggest challenge of your sector?** The food delivery market is growing and bringing more competitors onto the scene. As a result, we have to concentrate on setting new standards.
2. **How do you build your team?** By looking for people who pursue the same dream as we do. It doesn't matter whether someone has a university degree or has completed an apprenticeship. What is important for us is the fire for the cause.
3. **What does company culture mean to you?** We want to create a working environment in which people are happy to perform at their best. We also make it a point to indulge in the good life with staff bike rides, barbecues and office cooking sessions.

75.

Kogane-yu
Tokyo

**The third-generation owner drawing
a new look for a cultural institution**

Founded: 1932
Employees: 25
Length of renovation: 2 years

Yoga classes and vinyl records aren't typical
features of the traditional Japanese *sento*
(public bathhouse) but Takuya Shimbo is
doing everything he can to keep this beloved
slice of Japanese culture afloat. Shimbo is
the third-generation owner of Daikoku-yu,
a Tokyo bathhouse established in 1949,
and Kogane-yu, an older bathhouse five
minutes' walk away. At one time there were
thousands of *sento* in Tokyo but now that 95
per cent of people have bathrooms at home,
the customer base is shrinking.

Undeterred, Shimbo is showing that the
sento has a place in modern life. He started
with all-night openings and merchandise at
Daikoku-yu and then made the bold decision
to give Kogane-yu a radical makeover. For
all the raw concrete, blonde wood and fresh
tiling, Kogane-yu retains the core elements of
the classic *sento* – even the requisite mural of
Mount Fuji, here interpreted by young artist
Yoriko Hoshi. Other innovations include a
cypress-wood sauna, a craft-beer bar and an
exciting schedule of events.

Q&A with Takuya Shimbo

1. **What's the biggest challenge of your
   sector?** Finding the next generation to succeed
   a *sento* business. There is a set fee for public baths
   in Tokyo which is very low when you consider
   running and staff costs – making it difficult to
   attract people to work in the industry.
2. **How important is the community for you?**
   We want the business to contribute to the
   local community. For example, we do *yoku-
   iku* (bathing education) for local kindergartens
   and primary school kids. Almost everyone has
   a bath at home these days but the *sento* can still
   attract people and be a place for communication.
   At Kogane-yu we play records and serve beer.

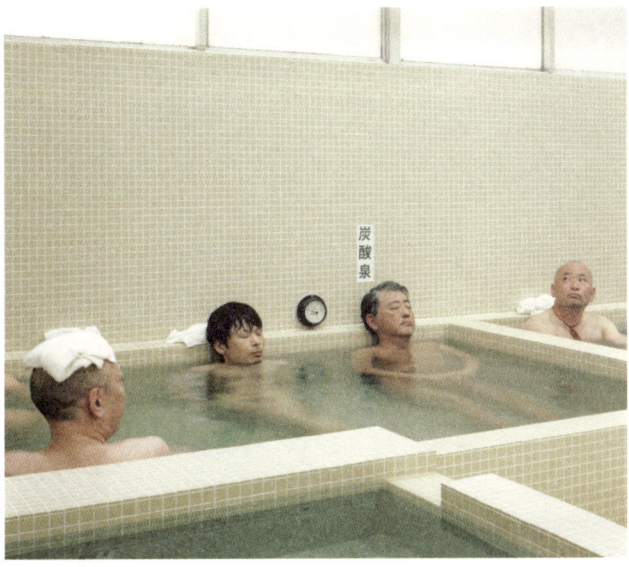

76.

93ft
Sheffield, UK

The family-run design studio on a mission to do it all

Founded: 2005
Employees: 20
Became profitable after: 2 years

Tim Hubbard, co-owner and co-creative director of 93ft, founded his interior design practice with brother-in-law Nick Clark in 2005 (*both pictured, Hubbard on left*). What began as a small branding and interiors practice has grown into an outfit that works across architecture, strategy, planning, websites, digital design and manufacturing. Hubbard, who has a background in industrial design and engineering, spotted a gap in the market for an agency that could provide its clients with the whole package.

Today, Hubbard runs the interior and manufacturing side of the business while Clark looks after branding and digital. Since its launch, 93ft has carefully transformed a number of spaces from The Pilgrm hotel in London (where the studio made almost 1,500 pieces of furniture) to the offices of the South Yorkshire Housing Association. "We're independent and we think about reclaimed materials, honest materials and giving the client bang for their buck. We try not to be part of fashion or themes," says Hubbard.

Q&A with Tim Hubbard

1. **What are the benefits of being based in Sheffield?** The city has a really creative feel thanks to its two universities. Nearly all our staff studied in Sheffield, many of which we nurtured from graduation. Plus, the quality of life here is magic – the Peak District hugs the city and you can be in the wilderness within 15 minutes.
2. **What advice would you have given yourself at the beginning?** I would tell myself to be bolder. If you have the right attitude and you work hard, you will always find a way.
3. **How do you build your team?** First we must like them, talent is second. Most of our team has worked their way up from a junior position.

77.

Pluto
London

The travel insurance that knew when and how to pivot

Founded: 2018
Employees: 4 (4 agency developers)
From idea to reality: 1 year

Alex Rainey and Harry Williams (*both pictured, Rainey on left*) started Pluto in 2018 as a re-thought travel insurance firm. But with the disruption that hit the sector in the following years, they knew their plans for branching out had to be stepped up a notch: today, Pluto functions as an efficient planning tool for a trip (from discovery to itinerary) and counts more than 12,000 users.

Bringing together their backgrounds in technology, design, product and branding the London-based founders had plenty of experience – but they needed external investment. "Securing investment can be the most exhilarating but also the most exhausting thing for a start-up," says Rainey. Despite initially focusing on insurance, "an old-fashioned market" that they felt they could change by making policies more flexible and personalised, the duo have now launched an app that works by collecting recommendations on destinations, and makes signposting locations for an upcoming trip much easier – and enjoyable.

Q&A with Alex Rainey

1. **What advice would you give yourself at the beginning?** Stoicism is an ancient philosophy which is applicable to today's noisy, messy, unpredictable world. Focus on the things that are within your control. It helps me be a calmer individual when it comes to decision-making.

2. **What are the challenges of your industry?** There is an abundance of start-ups in tech, many of which may be doing your idea. If it's a busy space, it might be hard to get investment or to get traction with users. If there aren't, then there's probably some question marks over why no one else is doing it. There may be good reasons for that, and there may be some bad reasons.

78.

Cut Salon Ban
Tokyo

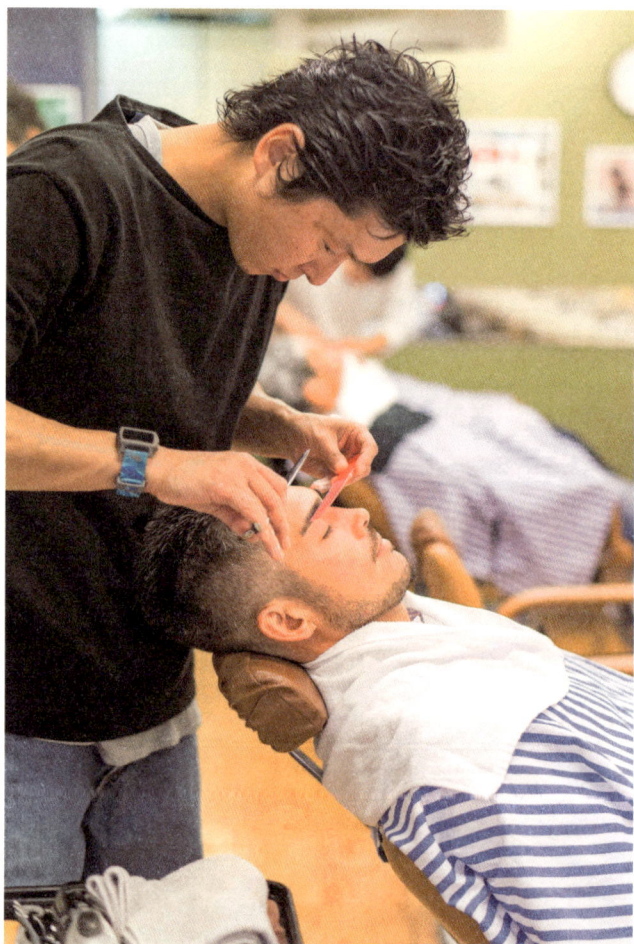

The Japanese barber shop that's a cut above the rest

Founded: 2002
Employees: 4
Number of customers per day: 50

Traditionally barbers have provided more than just a grooming service or a business proposition – they also serve the community with gathering places. Cut Salon Ban, a bustling five-seat barber in Tomigaya, Tokyo, is a great example. "Nobody hesitates to enter a convenience store or Starbucks whereas a barber is a closed entity," says owner Tsutomu Nagai (*pictured below, second from left*). "I wanted to change that perception. A lot of our customers come through word of mouth." When he opens in the morning, Nagai removes the front door and hangs a welcome curtain like an *izakaya* to make it more approachable.

Sure, Nagai's scissor skills and hot-towel treatments are key to Cut Salon Ban's success but it's the extra details that have cemented its role in the community: a blackboard in front of the shop displays a handwritten schedule of events taking place in nearby Yoyogi Park, which is printed out and distributed as a DIY newspaper. "We want to be of service to the people," says Nagai.

Q&A with Tsutomu Nagai

1. **What advice would you have given to yourself at the beginning?** Never say no. Be open and listen to your own customers. Great barbers have great customers who know the strengths and weaknesses of your service: you can grow your business by sincerely listening to them.
2. **What's the best thing about being your own boss?** Watching my staff grow. It's amazing to see them learn and polish their skills.
3. **What's the biggest challenge of your sector?** Finding the right staff. In our business, people are everything. We need to attract more young people into the trade.

79.
Rose
Paris

The creative agent matching talent to her tastes

Founded: 2007
Employees: 3
From idea to reality: 6 months

Olivia Mayolle founded Paris-based talent agency Rose in 2007. Today, she represents everyone from photographers and stylists to set designers, art directors and composers. She began her career in photo-editing with an internship at *Vogue* and went on to work for various Parisian photography agencies before deciding to bring together her own pool of snappers.

"I no longer wanted to sell artists who didn't completely match my taste," says Mayolle. "I've always struggled to put into words what draws me to an artist. I need to like the personality. And there needs to be a certain elegance in what they do." Mayolle is also keen to do things differently when it comes to running her own business. "The industry is so fast-paced, with artists coming and disappearing again within two years. As a reaction I'm building long-term relationships with the talent I represent. We function like a family, where all artists know each other and no one is in competition."

Q&A with Olivia Mayolle

1. **How is your industry changing?** More and more artists are returning to non-digital ways of working: shooting film and developing their own photographs. Print is making a comeback too.
2. **How have you grown your agency over the years?** I decided to branch out beyond photography, taking on people working in fields such as set design and music for fashion campaigns, allowing me to offer clients a full palette of artists.
3. **What's the best thing about being your own boss?** The daily contact with my artists. It's a relationship built on trust and affection. I know them inside out and they know me just as well.

80.

La Clinique du Jean
France

The tailor breathing new life into old denim

Founded: 2012
Employees: 2
Initial capital: €3,000

After looking in vain for a repair shop that could maintain his beloved jeans' distressed effect – but fix their malfunctions – French tailor Marly Manku decided to take matters into his own hands. He launched La Clinique du Jean in 2012. Today it provides a lifeline for all kinds of vintage and much-loved jeans with which his clients (collectors as well as passionate denim wearers) cannot bear to part.

Following his training with a Savile Row tailor, Manku cut his cloth at Levi's before settling in his studio now just outside Paris in Ivry. With his Union Special sewing machine he stitches tears and enlarges or shrinks jeans for a bespoke fit. An expert at reviving clothing from military to work-wear, he offers tailored customer service too: a quick phone call guarantees that he'll not only collect a garment but he'll also deliver it a week later looking as good as nearly new.

Q&A with Marly Manku

1. **How did you come up with the idea?** It was a service that I was looking for myself, and when I found it didn't exist, I decided to launch it.
2. **What advice would you have given yourself at the beginning?** Take a break – you'll be more effective. When I started, I barely stopped for several years. Even when I wasn't working I was thinking about the business. I thought that kind of dedication was good but I ended up making mistakes because I was exhausted.
3. **What's the best thing about being your own boss?** The ability to make quick decisions. You don't have to get approval from lots of different people before you do something.

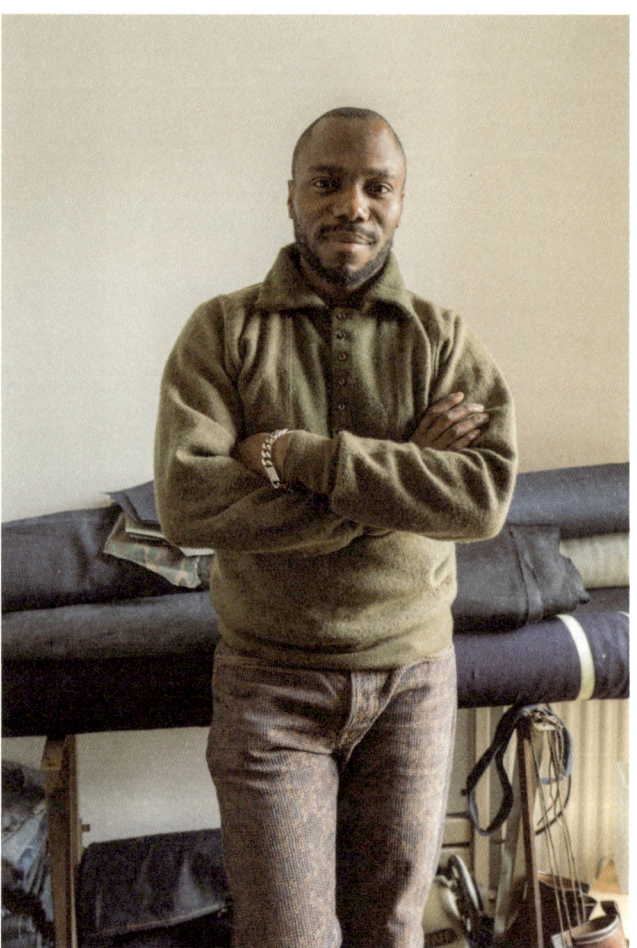

81.

Wardrobe Treatment
Tokyo

The Japanese drycleaners with an eye on service – not speed

Founded: 2018
Employees: 16
Annual turnover: €300,000

"Regular drycleaners would hesitate to take difficult jobs that involve delicate designer pieces or expensive materials," says Yoichiro Teramae. "But we don't say 'no' to our customers." Teramae, whose grandfather started a drycleaning business in Fukui, has been in the industry for over 30 years and has seen how, as fast fashion surged and people started treating clothes as consumables, the level of service in the market has dropped.

Going against the grain, Teramae opened Wardrobe Treatment to rescue everything from bespoke suits to treasured family kimonos. He charges about ¥3,500 (€26) to clean a shirt in three weeks, while the market average is about ¥300 (€2.20) in two days. Everything is shipped to Fukui, where a team of specialists select the right treatment then wash, dry and press each item. "In one transaction, customers need to come and see us twice," says Teramae. "Face-to-face communication is very important for us because we are looking after their clothes from the cradle to the grave."

Q&A with Yoichiro Teramae
1. **How long did it take for the business to become profitable?** About three years.
2. **What was your initial capital?** €114,000 for the web and shop, plus €228,000 for the specialist workshop in Fukui.
3. **What's the biggest challenge of your sector?** The competition among low-cost services is high because they can be copied relatively easily. They meet the needs of fast fashion, but our business caters to irreplaceable and memorable garments. Providing ultra low-tech services like ours involves risks and large resources, but as they can neither be automated nor done without skilled people, with patience they can become essential.

82.

Studio 33
Rome

The sound experts proving it's never too late to start something new

Founded: 2020
Employees: 6
From idea to reality: 2 years

Launched in late 2020, Studio 33 was founded by Crescenzo Abbate, his designer wife Ana Gugic (*both pictured, Abbate on right*) and a multi-skilled technical crew who provide discerning ears for all kinds of recordings – be they spoken-word or instrumental. "We're all 40-somethings," says Abbate (whose day job is running his own digital communications agency). "One morning I woke up and thought, 'let's pool our knowledge and share it in one space.'"

Operating in Rome's Trastevere district, Studio 33 covers everything from producing podcast series to working with internationally famed musicians. Inside, separate podcast and music recording suites, a kitchen-cum-catering area, dressing room and shower have all been impeccably installed to Gugic's plans; the mood is suitably industrial. What's more, the designer worked on a range of wooden horn-shaped loudspeakers made in collaboration with New York's OMA (Oswalds Mill Audio), which are stocked exclusively in southern Europe by Studio 33.

Q&A with Crescenzo Abbate

1. **What was your initial capital?** Around €1m, which we mostly used for buying up the space and investing in top-quality studio and audio equipment, as well as a few great design pieces.
2. **How did you come up with the idea?** I believe audio is the future and I've been incredibly inspired by the recent boom in podcasting. We are increasingly being submerged by screens and something as raw and simple as audio is a powerful tool.
3. **What does company culture mean to you?** I've realised the importance of gathering a group who share a passion. It's been fueling our growth and development more than anything else.

83.

The Fourth
Cape Town

The curators who turned their home into an art gallery

Founded: 2020
Employees: 7
From idea to reality: 5 months

Artist Rodan Kane Hart and interiors curator Maybe Corpaci never intended on turning their Cape Town digs into a temporary art gallery but when the pair took up residence in an apartment on the top floor of a six-storey art deco building in 2019 they converted the flat into a dual-use space – part home, part gallery. During the city's art fair, Hart decided to host the pair's inaugural exhibition aimed at offering emerging artists a platform in their own domestic environment.

In 2020, Hart and Corpaci developed a brand new gallery on the fourth floor of the same building, which they named The Fourth. They transformed it into an extension of the existing space upstairs, creating a place where collectors could browse pieces in a residential setting. Today, everything inside feels seamless. "We pride ourselves on re-engineering spaces and reimagining how they can function," says Hart.

Q&A with Rodan Kane Hart

1. **What are the benefits of being based in Cape Town?** Africa in general is an exciting place: it's a melting pot of culture and opportunity with boundless potential and incredible talent.
2. **What's the biggest challenge of your sector?** Creating an awareness around art and design and promoting it as intrinsic to culture and society. It also has high operating and production costs.
3. **What advice would you have given yourself at the beginning?** Draw up a business plan. Happenstance is great but setting things up properly from the beginning has long-term benefits.
4. **How long until you became profitable?** Four months.

84.

Richter
Moscow

The cultural institution showing you can be truly independent and make money

Founded: 2018
Employees: 26
From idea to reality: 1 year

"We want to create a community of people who realise that you must pay for good art and good service," says Anastasia Yefimova, founder and co-owner of Richter. It's a radical departure from the way that cultural institutions normally work in Russia: most are independent in name only.

But Yefimova dug into her savings and managed to draw together a small group of investors who believed in her idea: to combine a library, magazine shop, recording studio and art gallery with a luxury hotel and restaurant. Located in the heart of Moscow in a 19th-century mansion, Richter is the perfect marriage of hospitality and culture. Because hotel guests tend to be creatives, they take advantage of the in-house facilities. As Yefimova says, Richter is about creating "a self-contained experience". Most of the complex's revenue comes from the hotel and restaurant which helps sustain a cultural programme that includes concerts, talks, performances, DJ sets and exhibitions.

Q&A with Anastasia Yefimova

1. **How did you come up with the idea?** I realised that Moscow needed a place where you could not only have a comfortable stay but also record a music album, meet with journalists and simply hang out.
2. **What are the benefits of being based in Moscow?** In Russia people sincerely believe in new ideas, are easily inspired and will gladly help. We believe in miracles – that's why they happen.
3. **What's the biggest challenge of your sector?** It's a tough climate generally, but Richter is so multifunctional, we managed to adjust. When hotel stays were down because of lockdowns, we devoted part of the hotel to an art residency.

85.

Kana Kawanishi Art Office
Tokyo

The gallery owner who took her time to find the right path

Founded: 2014
Employees: 3
From idea to reality: 2 years

Kana Kawanishi is almost an accidental gallerist. Her career took many turns before landing her in a small space in eastern Tokyo. In fact, she worked in industries from fashion to telecommunications. Then publishing: she's been collaborating with New York's Rizzoli since 2006. Inspired by her work with the publishing house, Kawanishi came up with the idea for her own company: Kana Kawanishi Art Office was born with the aim of connecting Japanese artists with global publishers. "I felt that the reason there aren't many Japanese artist books out there isn't because of the quality of the artwork, it's that there was no connection," she says.

She soon realised that selling the works would also help her finances. At first she didn't think a physical space would be necessary but realised that "if you don't have a proper gallery, artists feel as if it's a one-night stand". Her roster initially focused on photography but today it spans wider – and she still brings out new titles on the side.

Q&A with Kana Kawanishi

1. **What was your initial capital?** One yen. I was very careful about running costs – when I started off, I shared the space with another gallerist. But we didn't split the physical space: I suggested we divide up the calendar instead. Every month we changed the sign – and that really worked.
2. **What advice would you have given yourself at the beginning?** Just a warm word that everything will work out. All the mistakes have to happen.
3. **What's the best thing about being your own boss?** It's more comfortable. All the stress and problems are caused by myself: some people would struggle with that sense of responsibility but for me it just makes sense.

86.

Sun Theatre
Melbourne

The cinephiles with an eye on the bigger picture

Founded: 2003
Employees: 50
From idea to reality: 2 years

In the Melbourne suburb of Yarraville you'll find the art deco home of the Sun Theatre – a cinema showing arthouse films and classics alongside the latest releases. Originally opened in 1938, the Sun had been left derelict for 20 years when owner Michael Smith took over in 1995. He began by operating a film society which proved so popular that he and his interior-designer wife Anne decided to restore the cinema to its fully functioning glory.

The secret to the Sun's success is in its staunchly community-centred approach: Smith was instrumental in creating a European-style piazza opposite the outpost, and he actively supports local businesses. Before every film, the cinema shows a short newsreel of Yarraville's highlights. "When people come here I want them to go to local cafés and restaurants, pick up a book next door," says Smith. It's no wonder that while the average Australian goes to the movies four times a year, the average Sun patron turns up 17 times.

Q&A with Michael and Anne Smith

1. **How did you come up with the idea?** We've always had a love of film – we would regularly attend other cinemas and think about how we could do it better, assuming (or hoping) that others would feel the same.
2. **What's the best thing about being your own boss?** Risk and reward – when we have a new idea we can just try it, tweak it and try it again. We do things because they are fun and we trust that the bottom line will follow.
3. **What does company culture mean to you?** The Sun is all about engaging with the community. We provide things at a fair price so that people return regularly – profit is the by-product, not the purpose.

87.

Primavera Sound
Barcelona

The festival founders dancing to their own tune

Founded: 2000
Employees: 100
From idea to reality: 2 years

What began in 2001 as a 7,000-spectator celebration of live music in Barcelona has grown to become one of Europe's premier summer festivals. Founded by Pablo Soler, Alberto Guijarro and Gabi Ruiz, it's become quite the gregarious get together. Today, together with its record label Primavera Labels, the company remains independent despite the growing influence that corporate capital (and ownership) has on the world's festival calendar.

Each year Primavera Sound attracts some 220,000 punters – half of whom make their annual pilgrimage from abroad – thanks to diverse headline acts such as Grace Jones, Sigur Rós and the Wu-Tang Clan. "When Neil Young played in 2009, that was a big moment for me," says Soler. "We'd been through a very tough few years because there was so much competition and we almost closed in 2008. But booking Neil Young was a massive boost. Barcelona had also just won the Champions League when he performed so he wore the team's scarf on stage."

Q&A with Primavera founders
1. **How did you come up with the idea?** In the 1990s Alberto and Gabi were programming the electronic line-up of two festivals [Benicàssim and Doctor Music]. Pablo was Gabi's lawyer and in 1999 the three of us started thinking about how we could run a better festival ourselves.
2. **What advice would you have given yourself at the beginning?** Your idea is great, even if you don't know it yet. We only began to see the light only four or five years after we started. Just be patient.
3. **What does company culture mean to you?** We always celebrate big moments together. It's the best way of growing a feeling of togetherness.

88.

Salut au Monde
Porto

The gallerist who's changing the landscape of cultural funding

Founded: 2019
Employees: 2
From idea to reality: 3 months

Before opening photographic gallery Salut au Monde in Portugal, Spaniard Pablo Berástegui held a raft of senior cultural management positions in his home country. "I was working on large, complex projects and felt that the moment had arrived for something more personal," he says. "I was managing big teams and big budgets but I was moving further away from the artists."

The precarious nature of funding in the cultural sector means that even big-name institutions struggle with cashflow. Berástegui's solution was to develop a strategy based on subscriptions rather than sales. In return for an annual contribution of €400, members receive a print from each of Salut au Monde's quarterly exhibitions. The model certainly has benefits: "I can take chances on what I exhibit. I am focusing on up-and-coming photographers rather than established names so we can help people get their work seen," says Berástegui. "It's about being part of a community that supports something interesting."

Q&A with Pablo Berástegui

1. **How did you come up with the idea?** I was inspired by Rafael Doctor's editorial project Los Doscientos. His idea was to produce artists' books and pre-sell them to a community of 200 interested parties, thus guaranteeing the viability of each proposal.
2. **What's the biggest challenge of your sector?** Many believe that collecting art is the reserve of the wealthy. I am more interested in inviting all sorts of people to consider buying an original print, by trying to keep prices under €2,000.
3. **What advice would you have given yourself at the beginning?** Keep things uncomplicated. The clearest, simplest approach is often the best.

89.
Four Brothers Drive-In
Amenia, New York State

The small-town drive-in cinema that revived an old, beloved format

Founded: 2013
Employees: 50
Initial capital: €820,000

In the town of Amenia, in New York state, you'll find the Four Brothers Drive-In – which was in fact launched by only two brothers: John and Paul Stephanopoulos (*both pictured, Paul on left*). Its name comes from their father's restaurant next door, Four Brothers Pizza. In 2012, John and Paul turned the land behind the pizzeria into a drive-in cinema. "We love movies and bringing people together," says John. "Plus there was no entertainment in the area." Today, customers travel from the neighbouring states and it's easy to see why: the space is surrounded by trees while the speakers compete with nature's chorus. And the food delivered to punters' cars helps too.

Having no experience in running this kind of venture, the first year was "pretty bootleg", says John. After investing in a digital projector and striking deals to show first runs, the venue now offers a high-end experience. Perhaps cinema's future won't be about big screen versus small; the windscreen could well be a factor too.

Q&A with John Stephanopoulos
1. **What are the benefits of being based in a small town?** Amenia is a hidden gem, tucked away, making it an adventure just to get here. It's not mainstream and it has small-town charm with a big personality.
2. **What's the biggest challenge of your sector?** Finding staff in our area is extremely difficult – being able to deliver all the extras we offer is very challenging in the entertainment industry when staffing is tricky.
3. **What's the best thing about being your own boss?** The excitement of being in the driver's seat; being able to dictate the future of something and really make an impact.

90.

Microqlima
Paris

The label owner nurturing France's hottest musical talent

Founded: 2014
Employees: 7
Annual turnover: €1m

Antoine Bisou always wanted to work in music but it took him years to think of it as a viable career path. Before dropping out of his politics degree he moved to Berlin in 2009 to intern for independent labels. Living in the city opened his eyes to the industry and convinced him to try and forge his own path within it. "When I came back I started DJing and organising parties and festivals," says Bisou, who worked as a graphic designer on the side until he began to earn money through his musical endeavours.

He became the manager of Parisian pop band L'Impératrice who were among the first signings when Bisou launched his own label. Today, Microqlima has just five acts on its roster but they're some of France's biggest hitters and include the likes of Isaac Delusion and Pépite. "I'd rather have fewer artists, take really good care of them and put more effort into making them successful," says Bisou. "We only sign one artist every two years or so but I still listen to demos every day."

Q&A with Antoine Bisou

1. **How did you secure funding?** At first I approached major labels looking for funding but the contracts they offered were terrible. In the end, an independent distributor helped me with funding and gave me the confidence to do it by myself.
2. **How do you build your team?** The most important things are attitude and teamwork. Someone might not have all the skills already but people can learn quickly. I'm an example of that – I picked things up as I went along.
3. **What advice would you have given yourself at the beginning?** Just try things and don't be afraid. You'll make mistakes but if you have the right spirit, it won't feel like a failure.

91.

Click and Grow
Tartu, Estonia

The green-fingered inventor growing more than just profits

Founded: 2009
Employees: 50
From idea to reality in: 5 years

Mattias Lepp has worn many hats throughout his career. A trained musician and orchestra conductor, he ran his own media and design agency, hotel and bicycle business before founding Click and Grow. The company, which is based in Estonia's second city Tartu, makes plug-in devices that allow users to easily cultivate everything from lavender to lettuce in their own homes. Growers insert specially-designed seed pods into a self-watering device with inbuilt LED lights that are engineered to stimulate growth. It's a slick, compact design developed with Nokia's former lead designer Mika Nenonen.

Lepp had been a keen inventor since childhood, and inspiration for Click and Grow struck after reading about how Nasa had found a way to grow plants in space. "The technology was so fascinating that I started to build my own devices at home," says Lepp. "Suddenly, during the cold Estonian winter, some tomatoes started to grow."

Q&A with Mattias Lepp

1. **What are the benefits of being based in Tartu?** The start-up ecosystem here is very good – companies like Skype, Bolt and Transferwise are all Estonian. There's also a high quality of life here.
2. **What's the best thing about being your own boss?** The most important thing for me is the creativity it allows me. I see making a good company like painting or making music. It's a form of expression.
3. **What does company culture mean to you?** Every year the team gathers to plant trees across Estonia. We want people from different parts of the company to connect with each other and with nature too.

92.

Tylko
Warsaw

The furniture-makers using augmented reality to sell custom-made pieces

Founded: 2015
Employees: 175
Annual turnover: €36m

Flatpack furniture is often associated with being fiddly, ill-fitting and faffy but that's a preconception that Polish furniture firm Tylko wants you to shelve. One of the most memorable orders that the team received was a 16-metre-wide bookcase for a chalet in the Swiss Alps – and they were able to deliver. "We are not a typical furniture business," says co-founder Hanna Kokczynska (*pictured*).

The trick is a nifty app that uses augmented reality to give customers more control over the design process without the hassle (and expense) of getting something completely custom-made. Users can build furniture – within certain parameters – that fits perfectly in their room, adjusting it on a phone screen until it looks just right and then ordering with the click of a button. The Polish-made products are built from plywood sourced from Northern European forests and delivered in flat packs – but with no tools required for assembly.

Q&A with Tylko co-founders

1. **What's the biggest challenge of your sector?** Poor quality of furniture and low prices has promoted a throw-away culture. Tylko only produces what has been ordered meaning we can offer bespoke furniture at an affordable price point.
2. **What advice would you have given yourself at the beginning?** Find partners who will stimulate you intellectually, who you trust and who are fun to work with.
3. **What does company culture mean to you?** As founders, we communicate openly with everyone at Tylko: our success numbers, our business strategy, our downfalls and urgencies so people can do their best to work on solutions.

93.

Dipulse
Svenljunga, Sweden

The entrepreneur refreshing existing technology for new gains

Founded: 2018
Employees: 12
From idea to reality in: 3 years

Innovation isn't always about making something new. Sometimes, it's just a case of finding a fresh way of using something that's already been developed. In 2016, Richard Statham came across neuromuscular electrical stimulation (NMES) technology, a common tool used in sports medicine to strengthen muscles by sending electrical shocks to different parts of the body. The electrode-wired gear was poorly packaged and anything but marketable but Statham immediately envisioned the possibilities.

A former jiu-jitsu fighter with a decade of experience working at Volvo, Statham brought the right contributors onboard – a London-based programmer, a Swiss engineer and a Taiwanese factory. In 2020, and 13 test versions later, they launched Dipulse's full-body Smartsuit. The app-controlled suit is intended to enhance physical performance for athletes of all stripes. But Statham is in talks with industry leaders of a range of sectors and the possibilities, he stresses, are endless.

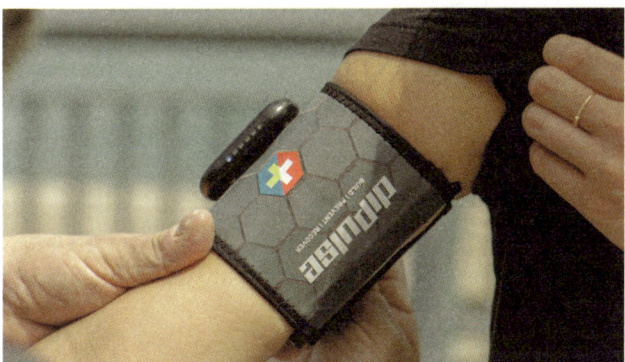

Q&A with Richard Statham

1. **What's the biggest challenge of your sector?** Our biggest challenge is that we are crossing two sectors – sportswear and technology. This is our USP but it also means we are entering a new market, one that isn't yet established. We are constantly learning as we go.

2. **What advice would you have given yourself at the beginning?** Don't be complacent about how important it is to get the message out there – explaining what you are doing to those outside the industry is the most important factor in any new company.

3. **The best thing about being your own boss?** Being able to pick the team and share their energy.

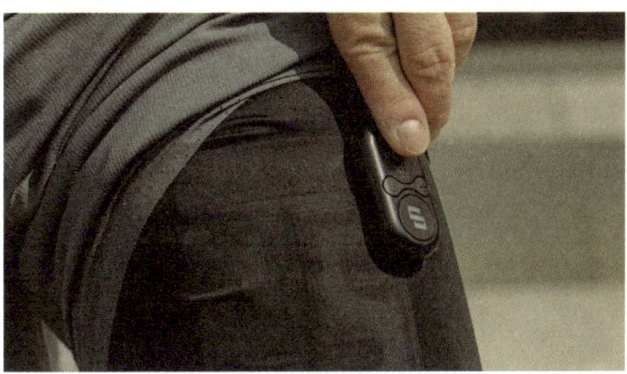

94.

Mellow
Tokyo

**The app that's connecting communities
and fueling a lunchtime revolution**

Founded: 2016
Employees: 34
Number of registered food trucks: 1,142

Mellow, a food and technology start-up,
has revolutionised the weekday lunch game
in Tokyo. In 2016, the company started to
fill a relative gap in the market, creating a
business platform for passionate food-truck
owners. Mellow connects mobile chefs and
property owners, helping the latter rent out
unused squares and carparks during lunch
hours. It's a win-win model: if you're a
building owner, a rotating army of food-
trucks (or kitchen-cars as they are known
in Japan) helps keep workers happy.

    Mellow also has a database for the
food-truck owners. The sales log from each
truck streams back to a central system and
members can see how many dishes each chef
has sold at a location, meaning they are better
able to estimate how much food to prepare to
minimise waste. They sign up for a location
on their preferred dates while customers
can see the whereabouts of their favourite
wagons in an app. Mellow also makes sure
everything from hygiene to fire safety,
parking and rubbish collection is dealt with.

Q&A with Mellow co-founders
1. **How long until the business became
   profitable?** About three months.
2. **What's the biggest challenge of your sector?**
   Although local municipalities give licenses to
   chefs to operate food trucks, it's still difficult for
   them to secure a location as it's illegal to occupy
   the road. There is a limit to what they can do
   individually to negotiate with property owners
   – that's where we step in.
3. **What advice would you have given yourself
   at the beginning?** Our business is built on
   trust with partner food-truck business owners.
   Nothing is more important than maintaining
   those relationships.

95.

Unu
Berlin

The trio bringing electric scooters to the masses

Founded: 2013
Employees: 75
From idea to reality: 2 years

Changing the way people move through cities is one of the central challenges of our times. In 2013, Mathieu Caudal, Pascal Blum (*both pictured, Caudal on left, Blum in centre*) and Elias Atahi decided that they wanted to play a part in the transformation so they founded Unu, an electric scooter start-up. "We'd lived in Beijing and other big Asian megacities, where we experienced the big challenges of urban mobility today, but also how light-weight electric two-wheelers can be the solution to it," says Blum.

Today more than 10,000 Unus fill the streets of cities such as Berlin and Paris, but the journey to this point wasn't always a straightforward one. "Founding a company is a rollercoaster," says Caudal. "Hardware development is extremely costly and time-consuming. Access to capital can also be a challenge. We became resilient; it helps you go through the hard times but it makes it difficult to enjoy the small achievements on the way."

Q&A with Unu founders

1. **How do you build your team?** We focus on building a diverse team in terms of personalities, backgrounds and experience – this helps us to challenge decisions and constantly improve.
2. **What does company culture mean to you?** A shared set of values that creates trust between all team members and lets everyone focus on what matters.
3. **What advice would you have given yourself at the beginning?** Don't get stressed if a plan doesn't work out or if you experience challenges. You will learn a lot from them and they will make you stronger. So stay calm and focused on the objective instead. Resilience is key.

96.

Blue Bird
Jakarta

The family firm embracing change and soaring to new heights

Founded: 1972
Employees: 30,000 (including drivers)
Number of fleets: 21,000

Blue Birds are a common sight in Indonesia. From Jakarta to Bali, some 26,000 drivers sit behind the wheels of the taxi firm's distinctive blue cars. The family-owned business, which was founded in 1972, runs everything from limousines to logistics – and it's become a national icon in the process. But the arrival of foreign ride-hailing firms threatened to knock it off its perch. So its president Noni Purnomo set about whipping the taxi operator into shape.

And she is succeeding: Blue Bird Group is now a modern, tech-savvy service provider. Changes have ranged from a new workplace to a partnership with domestic ride-hailing company Go-Jek. "We are moving upwards again and the worst is over, provided we keep transforming," says Purnomo. This includes exploring parcel and food delivery opportunities with online retailers that combine its taxi and logistics businesses. "Being around for so many years gives us strength but the way we do things has to be different."

Q&A with Noni Purnomo

1. **What advice would you have given yourself at the beginning?** Uncontrollable factors influence any organisation's performance – the ability to adapt quickly to change is crucial.

2. **How do you build your team?** By treating them as family – tough love! We strive to make a positive impact on society, starting with our own employees. With that in mind we have introduced a range of internal initiatives such as an empowerment programme for women and a scholarship scheme for our drivers' children.

3. **What's the biggest challenge of your sector?** Customer behaviour and demands for transportation are constantly changing.

97.

X Shore
Stockholm

The serial innovator making waves in the boating world

Founded: 2016
Employees: 60
Initial capital: €8.3m

Konrad Bergström is well acquainted with the highs and lows of being a business owner. He had huge success early in his career with a clothing distribution business, but the company folded and for a time Bergström was even sleeping in his car. Being the seasoned entrepreneur that he is, however, he dusted himself off and went on to enjoy huge success producing headphones and speakers.

His most recent venture is X Shore, an electric boat company launched in 2016. "When I throw the dice, I go all in," says Bergström. "I think you need that kind of mentality to succeed with innovative projects." The company makes fully modular pleasure craft equipped with electric motors that make for a quieter and more relaxed onboard experience, as well as lessening the harmful impact motorboats can have on their surroundings. "For me, it was important to provide a way for people to get out on the water without the noise and fumes that usually disturb wildlife and marine life."

Q&A with Konrad Bergström

1. **How did you secure funding?** I sold my old company. At that point, I could have probably kicked back and gone surfing but I've always felt the responsibility to be part of a positive change.
2. **What's the biggest challenge of your sector?** Driving the future of connected electric boats is always a challenge when you're the innovator, and not a follower, because everybody looks to us to set the standard.
3. **How do you build your team?** I don't tend to employ people that I would choose to hang out with on Fridays. I want people who are very different to me, who can bring outside knowledge and something else to the table.

98.

Mariposa
Toronto

The professional cyclists who decided to pedal in another direction

Founded: 2014 (originally 1969)
Employees: 4
Initial capital: €136,000

The seed for Mariposa Bicycles was sown in London during the Second World War. Its founder Mike Barry, who died in 2018, spent his childhood picking through bomb sites, finding old bicycle frames and metal-scraps and turning them into functioning bicycles. He founded Mariposa in Toronto in 1969. "Cycling for him was an escape," says daughter in law Deirdre Barry. Both Deirdre and her husband Michael Jr had successful careers as professional cyclists, with Deirdre winning silver for the US at the 2004 Olympic Games. So it seemed only right that the pair revive the family business.

"A lot of frame-builders tend to focus on building one or two types of bikes; track or touring or road, but they don't really cross over," says Deirdre. "We've always crossed into most disciplines; that's always been unique to us." Mariposa now produces some 50 bikes a year – each one of them unique. "We've kept the brand true to what it always was – and that requires a lot of one-on-one attention with the customer."

Q&A with Deirdre Barry

1. **What's the biggest challenge of your sector?** Currently it is the supply chain. But broadly speaking it is a highly competitive, mature industry with competitors that do not always work together or come to a consensus.
2. **What advice would you have given yourself at the beginning?** We had a huge learning curve: we understood professional cycling and bike design when we relaunched the business but we did not understand the constantly evolving bike industry. Learning is all part of the process.
3. **What's the best thing about being your own boss?** Being able to be adaptable and creative as the market shifts and opportunities arise.

99.
Nordic Seaplanes
Aarhus

The pilot who started an airline by finding a niche

Founded: 2016
Employees: 20
Biggest investment: €4m on a new seaplane

When not in the air, seaplane captain Lasse Rungholm is busy handling a 20-strong staff of captains, co-pilots and ground crew who make up Nordic Seaplanes, the company he co-founded in 2016. Following his passions, Rungholm rediscovered his calling on a family trip to the Caribbean, "I knew I didn't want to fly regular jets," he says.

As one of northern Europe's only seaplane operators, the airline offers daily 45-minute commuter flights between Copenhagen and Aarhus, Denmark's two largest cities. The alternatives are a three-hour train journey or jet services that take over two hours. Boarding a Nordic Seaplanes service, instead, requires passengers to check in just 20 minutes before departure, a short ride from either city centre. Having experienced steady growth since its founding, operating nearly full flights and offering sold-out sightseeing tours over the summer, Rungholm recently invested in a second seaplane in a bid to double the daily service and introduce routes to Sweden.

Q&A with Lasse Rungholm

1. **How did you come up with the idea?** It's always been hard to get from Aarhus to Copenhagen so I knew we'd have a customer base from the start. I thought about a helicopter service but it was an expensive undertaking and there's something about seaplanes that fascinates me – quite simply I wanted to bring them to Denmark.
2. **What's the biggest challenge of your sector?** The permits and regulations are a bit of a headache and there's so much competition you must always find new ways to attract customers.
3. **What advice would you have given yourself at the beginning?** If you want to make a million in aviation you need to start with two.

100.

Bookman
Stockholm

The Swedish duo lighting the way for city cyclists

Founded: 2011
Employees: 5
Became profitable after: 1 year

In the Swedish university city of Linköping, the most popular way to get around is on two wheels. It occurred to David Axelsson and Victor Kabo (*both pictured, Axelsson on right*), however, that only a few of their fellow students actually had proper bike lights to keep them safe at night. "We started a project that handed out lights for free," says Axelsson, "which we financed by finding sponsors who would put their names on them."

   When they moved to Stockholm after graduating in 2011, the duo realised their project had the potential to grow even further. "We took inspiration from a few other Swedish brands, including Ikea, who have found success by taking boring, everyday products and designing them really well," says Axelsson, who teamed up with a product designer to create a selection of bicycle lights with a slick Scandi spin. They quickly proved a hit with design-conscious cyclists and the brand has since branched out into urban visibility with reflectors to help runners and pedestrians stay seen on the streets.

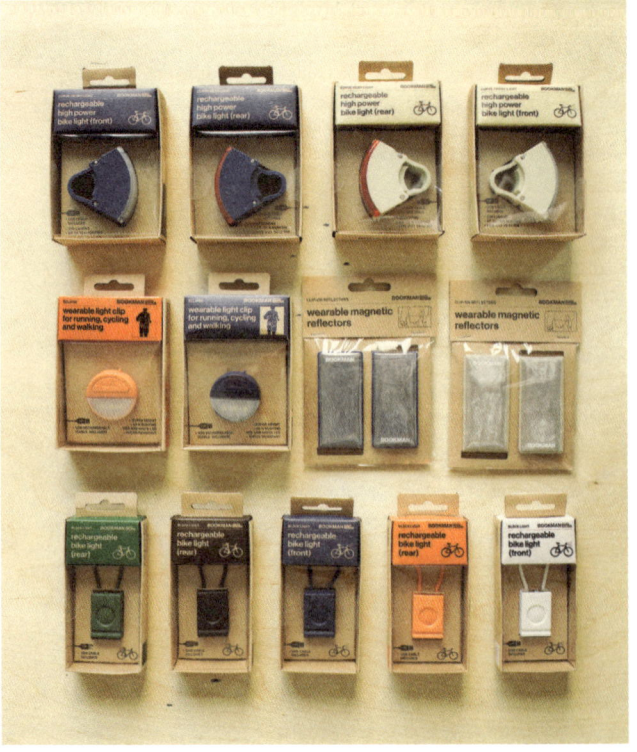

Q&A with David Axelsson and Victor Kabo

1. **How did you secure funding?** We only brought investors on board in 2019 – we needed some extra funds in order to focus on product development and grow the team. One of our investors is Stefan Ytterborn, who founded the helmet brand POC.

2. **What advice would you have given yourself at the beginning?** Don't spend a decade tinkering with a product and making sure it's 100 per cent ready before you reveal it to the market. It's better to receive feedback at an earlier stage.

3. **What are the benefits of being based in Stockholm?** Aside from all the amazing nature we have on our doorstep, it's a cool environment for entrepreneurs; especially when it comes to design.

Lots of factors go into the making of a successful business but the secret lies in grabbing an opportunity by the horns and taking that first, brave step.

Are you ready to do this?

Acknowledgements

The Monocle Book of Entrepreneurs

EDITORS
Joe Pickard
Molly Price

ASSOCIATE EDITOR
Chiara Rimella

DESIGNERS
Richard Spencer Powell
Maria Hamer

PHOTO EDITORS
Matthew Beaman
Shin Miura

PRODUCTION
Jackie Deacon

WRITERS
Abigail Abraham
José Miguel de Abreu
Jaroslaw Adamowski
Mikaela Aitken
Markus Albers
Liam Aldous
Genelle Aldred
David Allemann
Stefan Allesch-Taylor
Hamish Anderson
Chloë Ashby
Daniel Bach
Josie Baker
Sarah Balmond
Ravi Bapna
Sonya Barlow
Ruth Barry
Genevieve Bates
Aarti Betigeri
Peter de Boer
Robert Bound
Stacey Boyd
Emily Brooke
Petri Burtsoff
Ivan Carvalho
James Chambers

Annabelle Chapman
Anna Codrea-Rado
Brian Collins
Grace Cook
Francesca Cullen
Aiasha Dadral
Max Dautresme
Gabriele Dellisanti
Isabelle Dubern-Mallevays
Josh Fehnert
Lia Forslund
Verònica Fuerte
Amelia Gain
Ryan Gellert
Nolan Giles
Sophie Grove
Kenji Hall
Cynthia Hansen
Maria Hatzistefanis
Daphné Hézard
Will Higginbotham
Noor Amylia Hilda
Mary Holland
Yoshiharu Hoshino
Pip Jamieson
Elvire Jaspers
Helena Kardová
Will Kitchens
Alexei Korolyov
Camille Kriebitzsch
Josh Lachkovic
Rosie Lees
Ben Lewin
Tomos Lewis
Liv Lewitschnick
Kurt Lin
Trish Lorenz
Todd van Luling
Gaia Lutz
Hugo Macdonald
Kate Marlow
Antonia Märzhäuser
Tristan McConnell
Susie Mesure
Nina Milhaud
Leila Molana-Allen
Sophie Morris
Debbie Pappyn

Marie Perruchet
Lucila Pescarmona
Sofia Pescarmona
Joe Pickard
David Plaisant
Joann Plockova
Lizzie Porter
Molly Price
Venetia Rainey
Carlota Rebelo
Thomas Reynolds
Cyrielle Rigot
Chiara Rimella
Sarah Rowland
Laura Rysman
Ruchika Sachdeva
Marie Sophie Schwarzwer
Kim Scott
Ooooota Sebastian Adepo
Carlo Silberschmidt
Rob Smith
Richard Spencer Powell
Ed Stocker
Cherry Swayne
Alain Sylvain
Jiahui Tan
Julien Tang
Saul Taylor
Fernande van Tets
Shamil Thakrar
Junichi Toyofuku
Karina Tsui
Andrew Tuck
Hester Underhill
Justin Wang
Jamie Waters
Annick Weber
Julia Webster Ayuso
Fiona Wilson
Jasmin Yaya
Ed Yeoman
Anna Zaoui

PHOTOGRAPHERS
Marco Arguello
Mark Arrigo
Alex Atack
Yves Bachmann

Guillaume Belveze
Felix Brüggemann
Martin Bruno
Rodrigo Cardoso
Holly-Marie Cato
François Cavelier
Jimi Chiu
Jona Christina
Alex Crétey Systermans
Ana Cuba
Luis Díaz Díaz
Daniel Dorsa
Thomas Ekström
Luigi Fiano
Keisuke Fukamizu
Stephanie Füssenich
Víctor Garrido
Brian Guido
Mark Hartman
Elena Hetherwick
Thomas Humery
Alex Ingram
Kentaro Ito
Andreas Jakwerth
Kyle Johnson
Francesca Jones
Maria Klenner
Yurika Kono
Juho Kuva
Jason Larkin
Loi Xuan Ly
Levi Mandel
Julie Mayfeng
Benjamin McMahon
Lea Meienberg
Conny Mirbach
Ryan Murphy
Naoyuki Obayashi
Benne Ochs
Joey O'Connell
Tom O'Connor
Felix Odell
Dunja Opalko
Jonas Opperskalski
Hendrik Osula
Krzysztof Pacholak
Ian Patterson
Jussi Puikkonen

Evgeniy Rein
Tina Reiter
Ricky Rhodes
Robert Rieger
Ben Roberts
Tom Ross
Kevin Serna
Charlie Shoemaker
Jan Søndergaard
Landon Spears
Paulius Staniunas
Kohei Take
Peter Tarasiuk
Miwa Togashi
Brad Torchia
Stephanie Veldman
David de Vleeschauwer
Dan Wilton
Marvin Zilm

IMAGES
Alamy

ILLUSTRATOR
Kyle Metcalf

SPECIAL THANKS
Josh Fehnert
Amy Richardson

RESEARCHERS
Carolina Abbott Galvão
Alexandra Aldea
Audrey Fiodorenko
Julia Webster Ayuso
Zayana Zulkiflee

Monocle

EDITORIAL DIRECTOR
& CHAIRMAN
Tyler Brûlé

EDITOR IN CHIEF
Andrew Tuck

CREATIVE DIRECTOR
Richard Spencer Powell

PRODUCTION
Jackie Deacon

HEAD OF BOOK PUBLISHING
Joe Pickard

DEPUTY BOOKS EDITOR
Molly Price

ASSISTANT BOOKS EDITOR
Hester Underhill

DESIGNERS
Maria Hamer
Sam Brogan
Giulia Tugnoli

PHOTO EDITORS
Matthew Beaman
Shin Miura
Lucy Pullicino

Index

About Monocle

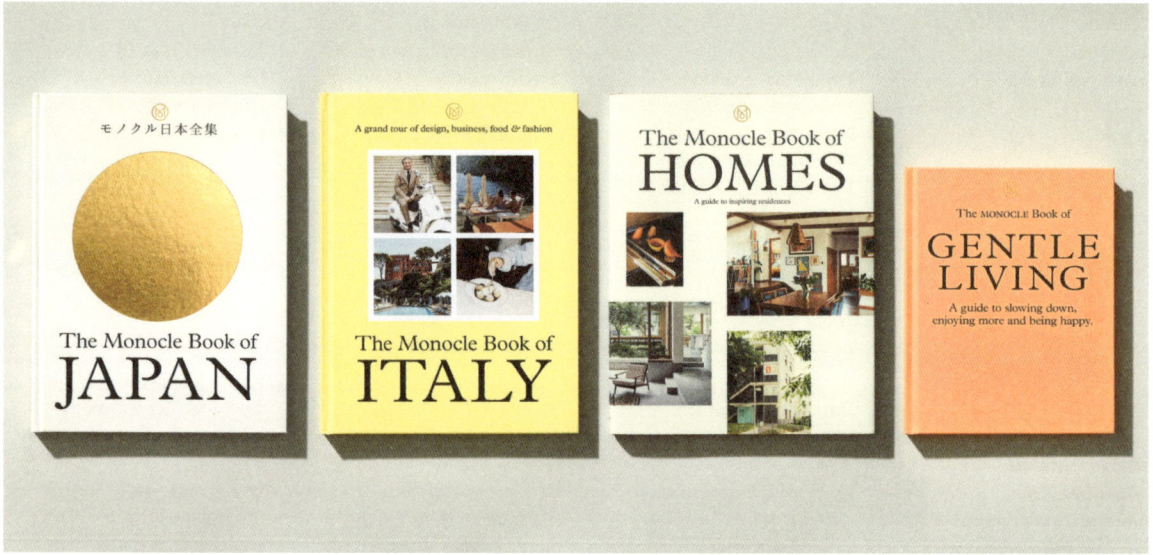

In 2007, MONOCLE was launched as a monthly magazine briefing on global affairs, business, design and more. Today we have a thriving print business, a radio station, shops, cafés, books, films and events. At our core is the simple belief that there will always be a place for a brand that is committed to telling fresh stories, delivering good journalism and being on the ground around the world. We're Zürich and London-based and have bureaux in Hong Kong, Tokyo, Los Angeles and Toronto. Over the years our editors and correspondents have met with countless entrepreneurs and business owners to find the secrets to success. This knowledge is unpacked in this book and throughout our reporting on Monocle 24, on our website and, of course, across our print products.

I.
Monocle magazine
MONOCLE magazine is published 10 times a year, including two double issues (July/August and December/January). We also have annual specials: THE FORECAST and two editions of THE ENTREPRENEURS. Look out for our seasonal newspapers too.

2.
Monocle 24 radio
Our round-the-clock internet radio station delivers global news and shows covering foreign affairs, urbanism, culture, food and drink, design and print media. You can listen live or download from *monocle.com/radio* – or wherever you get your podcasts. You may especially enjoy our weekly business show The Entrepreneurs.

3.
Monocle Minute
MONOCLE's smartly appointed family of email newsletters come from our team of editors and bureaux chiefs around the world. From the daily Monocle Minute to the Monocle Weekend Edition and our weekly On Design special, sign up to get the latest in lifestyle, affairs and design, straight to your inbox every day. It's all free too.

4.
Books
Since 2013, MONOCLE has been publishing books like this one, which follows in the footsteps of our best-selling titles *The Monocle Book of Homes* and *The Monocle Book of Gentle Living*. Our books are available on our site or at all good book shops.

Good luck